Family Bible Study

ADVANCED

BIBLE STUDY

COMMENTARY

SUMMER 2004
Volume 4 Number 4

"Your word is truth."—John 17:17

Study Theme
Body Life

Study Theme
That's Encouraging!

Study Theme

Peter's Principles for Successful Living

GENE MIMS, *Vice President*
LifeWay Church Resources

Ross H. McLaren
Editor in Chief

Stephen W. Carlson
Editor

Carolyn Gregory
Copy Editor

Stephen Smith
Graphic Designer

Carla Dickerson
Senior Technical Specialist

John McClendon
Mic Morrow
Adult Ministry Specialists

Send questions/comments to
  Editor, *Advanced Commentary*
  One LifeWay Plaza
  Nashville, TN 37234-0175
  Or make comments on the web at
  www.lifeway.com

Management Personnel

Louis B. Hanks, *Director*
Publishing
Gary Hauk, *Director*
Leadership and Adult Publishing
Ron Brown, Bill Craig, *Managing Directors*
Leadership and Adult Publishing
Alan Raughton, *Director*
Church Strategies

Acknowledgments—We believe the Bible has God for its author; salvation for its end; and truth, without any mixture of error, for its matter and that all Scripture is totally true and trustworthy. The 2000 statement of *The Baptist Faith and Message* is our doctrinal guideline

Unless otherwise indicated, all Scripture quotations are from the *Holman Christian Standard Bible®,* Copyright 1999. 2000, 2002, 2004 by Holman Bible Publishers. Used by permission. Scripture quotations identified as CEV are from the *Contemporary English Version.* Copyright © American Bible Society 1991, 1992. Used by permission. Passages marked NASB are from the *New American Standard Bible: 1995 Update.* © The Lockman Foundation, 1960, 1962, 1963, 1968, 1971, 1972, 1973, 1975, 1977, 1995. Used by permission. This translation is available in a Holman Bible and can be ordered through Lifeway Christian Stores. Quotations marked NIV are from the *Holy Bible, New International Version,* copyright © 1973, 1978, 1984 by International Bible Society (NIVmg. = NIV margin). This translation is available © 1989 by the Division of Christian Education of the National Council of the Churches of Christ in the United States of America. Used by permission. All rights reserved. Quotations marked NKJV are from *The New King James Version* copyright © 1979, 1980, 1982, Thomas Nelson, Inc., Publishers. Used by permission. Quotations marked NLT are from *The New Living Translation* copyright © 1996 and used by permission of Tyndale House Publishers, Inc., Wheaton, Illinois. All rights reserved. Quotations marked NRSV are from *The New Revised Standard Version* copyright © 1989 by the Division of Christian Education of the National Council of Churches of Christ in the United States of America. Used by permission. All rights reserved.

Family Bible Study: Advanced Bible Study Commentary® (ISSN 1526-5285) is published quarterly by LifeWay Christian Resources of the Southern Baptist Convention, One LifeWay Plaza, Nashville, TN 37234, James T. Draper, Jr., President, and Ted Warren, Executive Vice President, LifeWay Christian Resources of the Southern Baptist Convention. © Copyright 2004 LifeWay Christian Resources of the Southern Baptist Convention. All rights reserved.

Advanced Bible Study Commentary is designed for adults of any age who desire a study and application of Bible truths.

If you need help with an order, WRITE LifeWay Church Resources Customer Service, One LifeWay Plaza, Nashville, Tennessee 37234-0113. For subscriptions, FAX (615) 251-5818 or E-MAIL *subscribe@lifeway.com.* For bulk shipments mailed quarterly to one address, FAX (615) 251-5933 or E-MAIL *CustomerService@lifeway.com.* Order ONLINE at *www.lifeway.com.* Mail address changes to: *Advanced Bible Study Commentary,* One LifeWay Plaza, Nashville, TN 37234-0113.

Printed in the United States of America.

Meet the Writer

Kendell Easley wrote the lessons for this quarter. Dr. Easley is a graduate of John Brown University (B.A.) in Siloam Springs, Arkansas; Trinity Evangelical Divinity School (M.Div.) in Deerfield, Illinois; and Southwestern Baptist Theological Seminary (Ph.D.) in Fort Worth, Texas. Since 1988 Kendell has served as professor of New Testament and Greek at Mid-America Baptist Theological Seminary in Germantown, Tennessee.

Kendall is a frequent contributor to curriculum products for LifeWay Christian Resources. He is the author of several books, including *Living with the End in Sight*, *Revelation* in the *Holman New Testament Commentary* series, the *Holman QuickSource Guide to Understanding the Bible*, and *Illustrated Guide to Biblical History*, all with Broadman & Holman Publishers. Kendell also served as a reviewer for the *Holman Christian Standard Bible*.

Kendell and his wife Nancy are members of Germantown Baptist Church. They have one child, Jordan, a student at Wheaton College in Wheaton, Illinois.

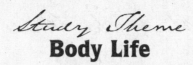
Study Theme
Body Life

What do you think of when you hear the phrase "local church"? Perhaps you recall a building with a steeple. Maybe you think of your pastor and the deacons or the staff. For some, members of their congregation may come to mind. A beautiful metaphor for the church in Scripture is a body—a living and healthy body with its many components working together for mutual benefit.

We all have seen examples of the human body when some of its parts don't work right. Sometimes babies are born with mental or physical disabilities. Perhaps one of our own limbs or organs has been injured. Despite astonishing advances in medical care, we all want our bodies to stay healthy and strong as long as we live. We wince when we hear about disease or injury or disability, whether to ourselves or to others.

So it is with a Christian congregation. We long to be part of a healthy church. We regret to learn about churches that aren't healthy. What does it take for a church to experience true body life? We will see that every member is important to a church's success. Every person in the church is to be committed to involvement in ministry opportunities. This brings glory to God and it benefits other believers as well.

This month's Bible studies examine four important aspects of healthy body life in the church. First, we will study baptism (June 6) as the initial experience shared by all members of a church. Second, we will consider the Lord's Supper (June 13), which is a shared experience of worship and fellowship with Christ. The third study draws our attention to the importance of godly church leaders (June 20). Finally, we will consider the important matter of spiritual gifts (June 27) as they affect every member of the congregation. Begin to pray now that God will use this study to bless your own life as well as the life of your local church.

BAPTISM

Bible Passages: Acts 2:36-41; Romans 6:1-10
Key Verse: Acts 2:38

❖ *Significance of the Lesson*

• The *Theme* of this lesson is that all Christians need to be baptized as an act of obedience to the Lord Jesus Christ.

• The *Life Question* this lesson seeks to address is, What makes baptism so important?

• The *Biblical Truth* is that Christians demonstrate their obedience to Christ and identification with Him by being baptized.

• The *Life Impact* is to help you appreciate the importance of baptism in the Christian life.

Why Study Baptism?

For many contemporary adults, baptism appears to be an odd religious ritual vaguely connected with Christianity. It is of little interest and doesn't seem to matter very much. Even Christians are exposed to a variety of teachings about baptism. Some claim that baptism is necessary in order to be saved. Others view it as an obsolete ritual propagated in legalistic circles.

Christians need to know that baptism is important for one's relationship to Christ and His church. This study emphasizes that the Lord Jesus expects all of His followers to be baptized in His name as a public proclamation of their loyalty to Him.

Word Study: *Baptized* (Acts 2:38)

Our English word *baptize* comes from the Greek verb *baptizo*, which is the intensive form of *bapto*, meaning "dip, immerse, or plunge under." In secular Greek, *baptizo* was rare and the noun form *(baptisma)* was not used at all. *Bapto* occurs only four times in the New Testament, always in the sense of dipping something in liquid, but *baptizo* occurs 77 times. In the New Testament, *baptizo* refers either to a religious ritual in which persons were immersed in water (Acts 2:38) or to a personal religious experience such as Spirit baptism (Acts 1:5). On one occasion Jesus used *baptizo* to describe His suffering and death (Mark 10:38).

John the Baptist baptized persons as a sign of their repentance (Matt. 3:11). Christian baptism not only symbolizes repentance and faith, but it also identifies the believer with the Trinity and pictures Jesus' death, burial, and resurrection (Matt. 28:19; Rom. 6:3-5).

❖ *Search the Scriptures*

After Jesus' resurrection and ascension into heaven, His disciples waited in Jerusalem according to His direction. On the day of Pentecost several days later, the Holy Spirit came on Jesus' followers in a powerful way. Peter preached the gospel to a vast crowd of people who were there for the festival. About three thousand people were saved and baptized that same day (Acts 2:41).

About 25 years later, Paul wrote his most famous letter. It was addressed to Christians living in Rome. Among many other things, he explained to them the meaning of Christian baptism. This ritual identifies believers with Christ and His death. In addition, baptism beautifully pictures that believers have been raised to life with Him.

An Act of Obedience (Acts 2:36-41)

What was the day of Pentecost as first-century Jews celebrated it? How can the boldness of Peter and the other apostles—who were so fearful and cowardly when Jesus was arrested and crucified—be explained? What does it mean to repent? What is the relationship between repentance, baptism, and the forgiveness of sins?

Verse 36: "Therefore let all the house of Israel know with certainty that God has made this Jesus, whom you crucified, both Lord and Messiah!"

After Jesus was crucified, His disciples lost all hope. Yet on the third day He arose from the dead. All four Gospels describe the empty tomb of Jesus. Furthermore, He appeared alive to His followers in a variety of places. One such location was a mountain in Galilee. There He met His disciples and gave them their marching orders: "Go, therefore, and make disciples of all nations, baptizing them in the name of the Father and of the Son and of the Holy Spirit" (Matt. 28:19).

Christ's disciples were acquainted with baptism because John the Baptist, Jesus' forerunner, had baptized people as a sign of repentance. Early in His own ministry, Jesus' disciples had baptized at His direction (John 4:1-2). Now Jesus directed that baptism become a permanent ordinance for all who have placed their faith in Him. It was to be performed in the name of the Trinity. Forty days after His resurrection, Jesus ascended to God's right hand (Acts 1:3).

The day of Pentecost—an annual Jewish harvest festival (also known as the feast of weeks) celebrated 50 days after Passover—became the first occasion for the apostles to obey their Lord's command. A great harvest of souls came to Christ. From that day until now, Christians have faithfully obeyed Christ's command to baptize those who believe the good news.

Acts 2:1-13 describes the miraculous coming of the Holy Spirit on the band of Jesus' followers in Jerusalem on the day of Pentecost. They were transformed into powerful, effective witnesses. The change in Simon Peter—who had so miserably denied Jesus the night of His trial—was astounding. Acts 2:14-36 summarizes Peter's bold sermon to the multitude of Jewish visitors in Jerusalem present for the holiday. Verse 36 concludes his message. The Jewish leaders had determined that Jesus of Nazareth had been a criminal worthy of death: **This Jesus . . . you crucified.** God's verdict was different. The Heavenly Father who raised Him had declared that He is **both Lord and Messiah.** He was the Lord who had fulfilled the scriptural prophecies about the coming Messiah. The resurrection proved this **with certainty,** and there were implications for **all the house of Israel,** that is, all Jews whether they were living in Judea or elsewhere.

Verse 37: **When they heard this, they were pierced to the heart and said to Peter and the rest of the apostles: "Brothers, what must we do?"**

This text is an early example of what Jesus' followers have experienced down through the centuries: The Spirit of God uses the proclamation of the Word of God to convict sinners of their need (John 16:8). Those in the crowd that day **were pierced to the heart.** Their minds and their emotions had been seriously affected, but they were not sure about the response they should make. Here is a reminder that knowledge about Christ and strong feelings concerning Him are not sufficient for conversion.

Verses 38-40: "Repent," Peter said to them, "and be baptized, each of you, in the name of Jesus the Messiah for the forgiveness of your sins, and you will receive the gift of the Holy Spirit. [39]For the promise is for you and for your children, and for all who are far off, as many as the Lord our God will call." [40]And with many other words he testified and strongly urged them, saying, "Be saved from this corrupt generation!"

The necessary counterpart to gospel proclamation is gospel invitation. Peter's response was forthright: **Repent.** This means to change one's direction or outlook. It could be translated "have a change of mind." They had been rejecting Jesus; now they were to trust Him as Lord and Messiah.

Peter also invited his hearers to participate in the outward sign of inward repentance and faith: **Be baptized . . . in the name of Jesus the Messiah.** By submitting to this symbolic action, they would indicate publicly that they were trusting in Him to forgive their sins and that they were confessing Him as the Messiah. Although a great crowd was present, the response had to be made one by one—**each of you.**

Acts 2:38 is commonly quoted by those who claim that water baptism is necessary in order to be saved. This view, however, rests on a misinterpretation of the relationship between **be baptized** and **for the forgiveness of your sins.** The challenge is to understand the preposition **for** (Greek *eis*) correctly. Admittedly in some New Testament instances, this word can indicate result. But the meaning here could also be understood as "because of" (see "at" in Matt. 12:41).

Another valid interpretation (preferred by this writer) is to study other New Testament instances where baptism and this preposition occur together. This has led many Bible students to conclude that a form of the Greek verb *baptizo* or the noun *baptisma* combined with the preposition *eis* always indicates *that with which the baptized person is being identified.* Here are four examples:

- In Matthew 28:19 baptized believers are identified with the name of the Persons of the Trinity.
- In Romans 6:3-4 baptized believers are identified with Christ and His death.
- In 1 Corinthians 10:2 the (metaphorically) baptized Israelites were identified with Moses.
- In 1 Corinthians 12:13 Spirit-baptized believers are identified with the one body of Christ.

In this way, Peter's statement in Acts 2:38 should be understood as a command to be baptized as a way of identifying with his message of repentance. On the day of Pentecost, that message was critical because some of those present had been directly involved in condemning and crucifying Jesus (v. 23). Being baptized symbolized that person's change of mind and heart about Jesus.

So far Peter had given two commands—**repent** and **be baptized.** His **promise** to those who obeyed these commands was that **you will receive the gift of the Holy Spirit.** The presence and power of God Himself would invade believers' lives, enabling them to live a holy life pleasing to God and to do all that He wanted them to accomplish. They would no longer live and work in their own strength. The promise was not limited to those present. It included not only **your children** (Jews) but also Gentiles, those **who are far off** (see Eph. 2:13,17). God's sovereign **call** to salvation in Christ over the centuries has included people from all nationalities and languages (see Rev. 7:9-10). It began with a Jewish gathering on the day of Pentecost.

Acts 2:40 indicates that only a portion of Peter's actual proclamation of the gospel is recorded. We also learn that his gospel invitation was passionate, for he **strongly urged them.** The generation of his day was especially **corrupt** because it had killed Jesus the Lord and would ultimately face divine condemnation. Individuals, however, still had an opportunity to **be saved.** Human nature hasn't changed, for our generation is also corrupt. But we can still use Peter's appeal in verse 40 to invite people to respond to the gospel.

Verse 41: **So those who accepted his message were baptized, and that day about 3,000 people were added to them.**

Those who **accepted his message** repented of their sins and trusted in Jesus. They now acknowledged Him as the Messiah. As a public confession of their faith they **were baptized.** Some have wondered how **3,000 people** could have been baptized so readily. But the city of Jerusalem, particularly the area around the temple, had a number of pools that could have been used for immersion. In any event, this text shows that from the very beginning those who trust in Jesus have been baptized in water as a symbol of their repentance and faith in Jesus as Messiah.

What lasting truths are in these verses?

1. Those repenting of their sins and believing in Jesus have their sins forgiven.

2. Water baptism identifies a person with Jesus and with the forgiveness of sins He provides.

3. From the first, new believers in Christ have been baptized in His name.

A Symbol of Death (Rom. 6:1-3)

Some people claim that if salvation is by grace then believers would live carelessly and not worry about sin. How would you respond to this charge? What relationship does water baptism have to your understanding of what happened when you were converted?

Verses 1-3: What should we say then? Should we continue in sin in order that grace may multiply? ²Absolutely not! How can we who died to sin still live in it? ³Or are you unaware that all of us who were baptized into Christ Jesus were baptized into His death?

Romans 6–8 contains Paul's explanation of the impact conversion to Christ makes in a person's life. He began his presentation by quoting an objection he had probably encountered as he had proclaimed salvation as the free gift of God's grace to undeserving sinners.

Since God's grace can cover the greatest of sins (Rom. 5:20), then wouldn't it be logical **to continue in sin in order that grace may multiply?** Wouldn't it be a powerful and impressive display of God's grace in our lives for us actively to pursue sinning so that His ongoing forgiveness would be evident within us? In other words, if all our sins are forgiven when we are converted, then what's to keep us from spiritual apathy in the Christian life?

Paul's first response is an emotional, **Absolutely not!** (See also 3:4,6,31; 6:2,15; 7:7,13; 9:14; 11:1,11.) In the rest of verse 2 the apostle asked a question which implies that believers are already in some sense dead to sin—and they need to realize it. If this is so, it is unthinkable that we should **still live in it.**

What did Paul mean that we **died to sin**? He did not mean that we are unable to respond to the temptation to sin, for believers plainly continue to struggle against sin throughout their lives (see Rom. 7:14-25). Rather, Paul meant that we are now dead to the tyranny of sin. Before our conversion, we were under the dominion of sin (3:9). Now that Christ has come into our lives, we are no longer under the power of sin. We have been liberated from sin, that cruel master that forced us into submission (see 6:17).

To drive home his point, Paul asked his readers to think about the common experience of believer's baptism that they had all shared. (Paul's reasoning here makes sense only if two things are true: first, all those who professed faith in Christ had been baptized in water; second, the form of baptism was immersion.) Paul asked, What did your baptism symbolize? Have you forgotten that **all of us who were baptized into Christ Jesus were baptized into His death?**

Every time we see a new believer plunged under the baptismal water, it reminds us of our own baptism. What is baptism except a symbol or a picture of an inward spiritual reality? When I repented and believed in Christ, I was joined spiritually to Him. Thus, in a sense, when He died and was buried, I died and was buried. I was **baptized into His death** in the sense that His death was applied to my life as the complete payment for my sins. The life that I lived before I was converted—hostile to God and disobedient to Him—is now over. I **died to sin,** and I was **baptized into His death.**

What lasting truths are in these verses?

1. No one who understands God's grace can want to continue to sin.

2. The beginning of the Christian life should be recognized as a death to sin.

3. Baptism symbolizes a believer's union with Christ in His death.

A Symbol of Life (Rom. 6:4-10)

*In addition to death, what does baptism picture? Why is it good news for believers to learn that they have been crucified with Christ? How is a believer set free from slavery to sin? What does **lives to God** mean?*

Verses 4-5: Therefore we were buried with Him by baptism into death, in order that, just as Christ was raised from the dead by the glory of the Father, so we too may walk in a new way of life. ⁵For if we have been joined with Him in the likeness of His death, we will certainly also be in the likeness of His resurrection.

Many people think that death ends everything. Those who know that **Christ was raised from the dead** understand that death can be the gateway to resurrection life. Jesus died and was buried, but that was not the end. **By the glory of the Father,** He was raised forever. The **glory** of God is the display of His many perfections. God is perfect in power, and by His mighty power Christ was raised forever. He was the first to **walk in a new way of life.**

The "death" of believers in baptism, therefore, is not the end but a door to new life. The waters of baptism symbolize that **we were buried with Him.** We were united to Christ in His death when we believed in Him for our salvation. We did not stay dead, however. We were also raised to **walk in a new way of life.** As believers, we need not wait for the resurrection of the body (at Christ's return) to experience the **glory of the Father.**

The sentence structure of verse 5 requires us to ask whether the condition has in fact happened. Have we **been joined with Him in the likeness of His death**? If we are believers, the answer must be yes (v. 3). If the condition has been met in us—as baptism certainly portrays—then it is certain that **we will certainly also be in the likeness of His resurrection.** Bible students have pondered whether the **resurrection** here refers to the believer's experience of new life *now* or to the believer's receipt of the resurrection body *at Christ's return.* The use of the future tense suggests that Paul was thinking primarily of the future, especially since Christ's bodily resurrection is in view. In some sense, however, believers have already started to walk **in a new way of life.** Paul prayed for the Ephesian Christians to know "the immeasurable greatness of His power to us who believe, according to the working of His vast strength." (Eph. 1:19-20).

Verses 6-7: **For we know that our old self was crucified with Him in order that sin's dominion over the body may be abolished, so that we may no longer be enslaved to sin, [7]since a person who has died is freed from sin's claims.**

One of the greatest challenges in the Christian life is overcoming temptation. These verses describe graphically the kind of change that happens in the life of a sinner who repents and trusts Christ. Paul had been portraying conversion as an experience of death, burial, and resurrection in union with Christ. Now he specified this death as the **old self** having been **crucified.** The words **old self** refer to the unconverted, sinful person I was before conversion. That old self died when I was born again, for "if anyone is in Christ, there is a new creation" (2 Cor. 5:17). The new self no longer has to give in to **sin's dominion over the body.** Believers continue to fight against sin, but the fight is now winnable. **Sin's dominion** can now **be abolished.** The Greek word for **abolished** does not mean "destroyed" but rather "made powerless." Sin still tempts a believer, but Christians **no longer** have to **be enslaved to sin** because its power is now inoperative.

One way to picture this is to imagine a prison cell in which the locks no longer work. The locks haven't been destroyed, but the mechanism is broken. Those who once were imprisoned behind locked bars can now walk out free. Before Christ came into our lives, we were **enslaved to sin.** Now we have been united to Christ by repentance and faith. We have **died** in union with Him. We are **freed from sin's claims.** We can walk out from the imprisonment to sin we once had. Baptism in water is a beautiful picture of being set free in this way.

Verses 8-10: **Now if we died with Christ, we believe that we will also live with Him, [9]because we know that Christ, having been raised from the dead, no longer dies. Death no longer rules over Him. [10]For in that He died, He died to sin once for all; but in that He lives, He lives to God.**

In verses 6-7 Paul's focus was on the result of conversion, particularly *the practice of sin.* How can we continue to sin when we understand our union with Christ, symbolized by our baptism? We have been crucified and buried. We are now new creatures in Christ. Sin has been defeated so that we are no longer enslaved to its cruel power. Now Paul shifts attention to think of the result of conversion related to *the power of death.* Paul wanted the Roman Christians to understand that death has been defeated just as surely as sin has been defeated.

For a brief period of time, between Jesus' death on Good Friday and His resurrection on Easter, **death** ruled **over Him.** By the mighty power of God, Christ's death was reversed. He was **raised from the dead.** Never again can death express any power over Him. Again, think about how water baptism pictures this experience. The Author of our salvation is gloriously alive forever, absolute proof that He is powerfully working to bring all those united to Him to full salvation.

Christ's death was a death **to sin once for all.** His death occurred not because He sinned but in order to bear the penalty of sin. His death showed how far God went in procuring salvation. As painful and grievous as Christ's crucifixion was, it happened **once for all.** The benefits secured by His death are freely provided to all who believe.

In His resurrection life, **He lives** forever. Never again can He die. **He lives to God,** that is, to the glory of God. The resurrection of God's Son stands forever as the most magnificent display of the greatness of God. The newness of life that we now experience as baptized believers is also meant to display our living to the glory of God—a display of His greatness and grace to us. When we are at last raised and we receive our resurrection bodies, that too will be an incredible display of God's glory. We—along with our Lord—will live forever as expressions of God's power.

What lasting truths are in these verses?

1. Christian baptism symbolizes a believer's union with Christ in His resurrection.

2. Sin's former dominion can be recognized as rendered inoperative in the life of believers.

3. Christians may experience resurrection life here and now as they live with Christ.

4. Christ's resurrection testifies that death has been defeated for all who are united with Him.

❖ Spiritual Transformations

The *Life Question* this lesson seeks to address is, What makes baptism so important? The answer has come from an examination of two passages. When Peter preached on Pentecost, the response of his hearers to his gospel invitation shows that from the beginning Christians have proclaimed that forgiveness for sins is possible only through repentance and faith in Jesus. This inward experience of forgiveness has always been expressed outwardly by water baptism. Paul explained to the Roman believers that baptism pictures the spiritual union of a believer with Christ. It shows that believers have been united to Christ's own experience of death, burial, and resurrection.

How would you now answer the Life Question for this study?
_____

*Whom do you know that may be confused about baptism and with whom you might share this message?*_____

*Can you remember the time and place of your baptism? Write the time and place here, as best you remember.*_____
_____

*If you have never been scripturally baptized, what should you do about it?*_____

Prayer of Commitment: *Lord Jesus, Thank You for your death, burial, and resurrection. Thank You that by repentance and faith I have the forgiveness of sins. Thank You for water baptism, which pictures my death to sin and resurrection to new life in union with you. Amen.*

THE LORD'S SUPPER

Background Passages: Matthew 26:17-30; 1 Corinthians 11:17-34
Focal Passages: Matthew 26:26-29; 1 Corinthians 11:23-32
Key Verse: 1 Corinthians 11:26

❖ *Significance of the Lesson*

• The *Theme* of this lesson is that all Christians need to understand the significance of the Lord's Supper and to partake of it on a regular basis.
• The *Life Question* this lesson seeks to address is, What significance does the Lord's Supper have for me and for my church?
• The *Biblical Truth* is that Christians demonstrate their love for Christ and unity with one another by partaking of the Lord's Supper together on a regular basis.
• The *Life Impact* is to help you consistently partake of the Lord's Supper in a manner worthy of Christ.

Why Study the Lord's Supper?

For some believers the Lord's Supper can become an empty ritual. Some congregations emphasize weekly or very frequent participation—and familiarity can lead to indifference. For many other Christians the Lord's Supper may have become so sporadic that they neglect it. Interestingly, Scripture contains no direct teaching on how often the Lord's Supper should be observed.

The New Testament focuses on what the Lord's Supper means. The Lord's Supper contributes to the unity of the church, the body of Christ. This study emphasizes that all believers should be committed to partaking of the Lord's Supper in a manner worthy of Him.

Word Study: *Unworthy way* (1 Cor. 11:27)

"Unworthy way" (1 Cor. 11:27) is a great translation for the Greek adverb *anaxios*, which occurs only here in the New Testament. The related adjective occurs only once also (1 Cor. 6:2). Both of these are negative forms taken from a verb meaning "consider worthy."

The related positive adverb occurs six times in the New Testament (Rom. 16:2; Eph. 4:1; Phil. 1:27; Col. 1:10; 1 Thess. 2:12; 3 John 6). Although believers were unworthy of forgiveness and the experience of God's grace because of sin, they are now to live in a manner that shows the highest regard for all that God has done for them. Thus, Paul asked the Philippians to "live your life in a manner worthy of the gospel of Christ" (Phil. 1:27). Similarly, Paul used the negative form to warn the Corinthians not to participate in the Lord's Supper in an unworthy manner.

❖ *Search the Scriptures*

On the night that the Lord Jesus was betrayed and arrested, He shared His last meal—a Passover meal—with His disciples. He took two of the customary menu items, the bread and the cup, and invested them with new symbolism, showing the disciples the spiritual meaning of His coming death.

Over 20 years later, Paul addressed a letter to Christians living in Corinth. He shared with them the Christian meaning of the Lord's Supper as an ordinance they were to continue observing. This ritual of worship commemorates Christ's death for sin until He returns. Paul challenged the Corinthians to understand that the Lord's Supper contributes to the unity of the church and that they should partake, but only in a manner worthy of Christ.

Instituted by Christ (Matt. 26:26-29)

*What was the meaning of Passover for the Jews? Why did Jesus take elements from a Passover meal to invest with new significance? What covenant did Jesus have in mind when He spoke of the **blood of the covenant**? What time was Jesus thinking of when He spoke of drinking again in His **Father's kingdom**?*

Verses 26-28: As they were eating, Jesus took bread, blessed and broke it, gave it to the disciples, and said, "Take, eat; this is My body." [27]Then He took a cup, and after giving thanks, He gave it to them and said, "Drink from it, all of you. [28]For this is My blood of the covenant, which is shed for many for the forgiveness of sins."

Passover was the annual springtime festival in which the Jews remembered that they had been set free from slavery in Egypt under Moses' leadership (Ex. 12:1-11). In Jesus' time, as well as today, the ritual meal included roasted lamb, unleavened bread, the fruit of the vine, and other items. Jesus asked His disciples to prepare such a dinner for Himself and the Twelve (Matt. 26:17-20). **As they were eating,** Jesus drew the attention of the Twelve from the past (the exodus from Egypt) to the future (His coming death).

The Lord knew that He was about to die by crucifixion and that His death would be "a ransom for many" (Matt. 20:28; see also vv. 17-19). He knew that John the Baptist had called Him "the Lamb of God, who takes away the sin of the world" (John 1:29). He did not, however, select the meat of the Passover to infuse with new meaning. Instead, **Jesus took bread, blessed and broke it,** and **gave it to the disciples.** The unleavened bread of the Passover was already present on the dinner table. His prayer of blessing surely put the disciples on notice that something unusual was about to happen.

Jesus' next words would have been even more startling: **Take, eat; this is My body.** Of course, His physical body was still present with them in the room, so He did not mean that the bread had turned into His body. Rather, the bread represented His body, which was about to be sacrificed on the cross. Just as bread must be eaten individually—nobody can eat for another—so Jesus' death must be received individually.

While they were still at the table, Jesus **took a cup** that had some of the Passover wine in it. According to longstanding Jewish tradition this cup was drunk after the Passover meal ended. This was probably what Jesus used that night. Just as Jesus had done with the bread, so He did with the cup: He gave **thanks** to God. Then He **gave it to them** so they could all **drink from it.**

Jesus gave a fuller interpretation of the symbolic meaning of the cup than He had with the bread. His first words, **This is My blood,** were similar to His earlier words about the bread. Again it must be noted that Jesus' physical blood was still present in His body there in the room, so He did not mean that the wine had turned into His blood. Rather, the wine represented His blood, which was about to be shed on the cross. Just as a beverage must be partaken of personally—nobody can drink for another—so Jesus' death must be received individually.

Next, however, Jesus said that His blood was the **blood of the covenant, which is shed for many.** This was a reminder that God's covenants of old were established by the shedding of blood (see Ex. 24:8, KJV). Jesus now said that His shed blood would establish this covenant. The phrase **for many** shows that Jesus died in the place of sinners—what is often called His "substitutionary atonement."

Jesus was aware that His death was God's ordained means **for the forgiveness of sins.** Throughout the Old Testament, but especially in the Book of Leviticus, the sacrificial shedding of an animal's blood was God's requirement for approaching Him. Now, however, everything the animal sacrifices had been pointing to—the death of the perfect Lamb of God—was about to be fulfilled. As the writer to the Hebrews later explained it, the Lord Jesus "after offering one sacrifice for sins forever, sat down at the right hand of God" (Heb. 10:12; see also v. 4).

Verse 29: **"But I tell you, from this moment I will not drink of this fruit of the vine until that day when I drink it new in My Father's kingdom with you."**

Jesus knew that He was about to pass through death's door, His blood spilled out and His body offered as a holy sacrifice. He would not have any further opportunity to **drink of this fruit of the vine** until He had tasted death and God had vindicated Him by bringing Him to life again. Although the disciples present that night were surely frightened and confused by Jesus' words, they may have remembered His confident promise that He would certainly **drink it new in My Father's kingdom with you** (compare Luke 22:30).

What lasting truths are in these verses?

1. Jesus initiated the Lord's Supper as a way of remembering His body and blood.

2. Jesus understood that His blood was to be shed in order to provide forgiveness of sins.

3. Jesus' promise to "drink it new" in His Father's kingdom demonstrated His confidence in His coming resurrection.

Reminder to the Church (1 Cor. 11:23-26)

How do we know that the Lord's Supper is for us rather than just a one-time occurrence? How does celebrating the Lord's Supper look back to the past? How does it look forward to the future? What does it ***proclaim*** *in the present?*

Verses 23-24: **For I received from the Lord what I also passed on to you: on the night when He was betrayed, the Lord Jesus took** bread, ²⁴gave thanks, broke it, and said, "This is My body, which is for you. Do this in remembrance of Me."

Paul had founded the Corinthian church during his second missionary journey. God had blessed the congregation with many converts. Several years later Paul learned that the church in Corinth had been plagued with many problems since he left, including divisions, immorality, and questions about congregational worship.

One of their problems focused on the way the members were abusing the Lord's Supper. Paul had learned that even at the Lord's Supper there were "divisions" among them (1 Cor. 11:18). Evidently some were using the Lord's Supper as an occasion for gluttony and drunkenness; other were being left out entirely (vv. 21-22). Paul's instructions were a severe warning for the church to get back on track. He reminded them first about the historical origins of the Lord's Supper.

Paul's teaching was no invention. He had **received** it **from the Lord** and had **also passed** it **on to you**. We are not sure whether Paul meant he had received this by direct revelation from Christ (see Gal. 1:12) or indirectly through the apostles (see 1 Cor. 15:3). Either way, Paul had absolutely reliable information about the origins of the Lord's Supper.

Paul did not emphasize that the Lord's Supper started as a Passover meal; rather, he focused on the solemn fact that it began **on the night when He was betrayed.** Matthew, Mark, and Luke (the three Gospels that report Jesus' institution of the Lord's Supper) all agree on this detail. Paul also knew that Jesus had begun with the **bread,** which He **broke.** The verb **gave thanks** is slightly different from the verb Matthew used ("blessed"). It translates the Greek verb *eucharisteo*, "I thank." (Some denominations use the name *Eucharist* as an alternate term for the Lord's Supper.) The general practice of Christian congregations throughout the centuries has been to include a prayer of thanksgiving to God for the bread and the cup as a part of the Lord's Supper, based on Paul's teaching in 1 Corinthians.

Luke's account also includes the words, **Do this in remembrance of Me** in reference to eating the bread (Luke 22:19). This provides evidence that Jesus ordained the Lord's Supper as a permanent part of what believers are to do, just as He had ordained baptism. The form of the words **in remembrance of Me** suggests actively calling something to mind, rather than just a passing recollection. For example, the Jewish Passover was an annual memorial meal in which Jews solemnly remembered their deliverance from bondage in Egypt (Ex. 12:14).

Here Jesus was instituting the Lord's Supper as a way for believers to remember their deliverance from the bondage of sin because His body was given up to death on the cross.

Verses 25-26: In the same way He also took the cup, after supper, and said, "This cup is the new covenant in My blood. Do this, as often as you drink it, in remembrance of Me." [26]For as often as you eat this bread and drink the cup, you proclaim the Lord's death until He comes.

Paul essentially repeated what the Gospels report about Jesus taking **the cup, after supper.** Paul paralleled the wording used by Luke, particularly including the word "new" in the phrase **new covenant in My blood** (Luke 22:20). Jeremiah had prophesied about the day when God would make a "new covenant" with His people (Jer. 31:31-34). Jesus was claiming that through His death God would establish the new covenant promised centuries earlier (see also Heb. 8:1-13; 9:15; 12:24).

Jesus told His disciples that night that they were to **do this . . . often.** How often is often? Jesus did not say. The Passover meal, occurring annually, could be thought of as "often." Likewise there is some evidence that in the Book of Acts "often" means weekly observances of the Lord's Supper (Acts 2:42; 20:7). Many Baptists have observed the Lord's Supper monthly or quarterly. Whenever we do it, above all it should be **in remembrance of Me,** words frequently inscribed on the Lord's Supper tables in churches. Only Paul reported that Jesus used the words **in remembrance of Me** concerning the cup. Perhaps Paul felt that the unruly Corinthians needed a repeated statement that the Lord's Supper is to remember *Him,* not to satisfy *human appetites*.

Not only does the Lord's Supper look back to **the Lord's death,** but it also looks forward to His coming. It reminds us that He will return in glory. Churches are expected faithfully to celebrate the Lord's Supper **until He comes.**

Thus Paul taught that **as often as you eat this bread and drink the cup,** there is a look back at the past **(the Lord's death)** and a look ahead to the future **(He comes).**

In addition, there is something special that happens in the present. Paul said that the very act of partaking of the Lord's Supper is one way to **proclaim** Christ's death. The Greek verb for **proclaim** occurs several times in Acts and in Paul's epistles to refer to the preaching of the gospel (see also 1 Cor. 2:1; 9:14). Thus, when the Lord's Supper is rightly observed, the gospel message is being proclaimed symbolically.

When believers gather to partake of the Lord's Supper, we should be deliberately focused on what we are doing. It is a proclamation in the *present* of the most important event in the *past* (Christ's death) until the most important event in the *future* (the coming of Christ in glory). Truly the Lord's Supper portrays the essence of the gospel.

What lasting truths are in these verses?

1. Churches can be confident of the historical origin of the Lord's Supper.

2. Jesus wants us to celebrate the Supper in remembrance of Him.

3. Christ explained that His death was the means by which the new covenant was established.

4. The Lord's Supper is to be observed often as a way of proclaiming the Lord's death until He returns.

Opportunity for Examination (1 Cor. 11:27-32)

Why is it important to evaluate ourselves before we observe the Lord's Supper? What are the spiritual results of taking the Lord's Supper in an unworthy way? What might be the physical results?

Verses 27-28: Therefore, whoever eats the bread or drinks the cup of the Lord in an unworthy way will be guilty of sin against the body and blood of the Lord. ²⁸So a man should examine himself; in this way he should eat of the bread and drink of the cup.

Some of the Corinthian Christians had been eating and drinking **in an unworthy way.** Their divisive spirit, their gluttony, and their drunkenness showed that they had little regard for the historical **body and blood of the Lord,** represented in the elements of the Lord's Supper. His body and blood had secured their salvation. Their contempt for what was sacred meant they were **guilty of sin.** It did not matter whether they were rich or poor, leaders or laypeople; **whoever** ate or drank **in an unworthy way** was **guilty.**

The only other New Testament passage to use the phrase **cup of the Lord** is 1 Corinthians 10:21, which is also the only New Testament text to use the phrase "the table of the Lord" or "the Lord's table" to refer to the Lord's Supper. All these phrases are reminders that this commemoration is to focus on Him. It is **the body and blood of the Lord** that we should remember. It is His cup, His supper, and His table. We are the invited guests, and we are present only by His gracious invitation. We should therefore take care to prepare to eat and drink in a way that pleases our unseen Host.

Paul urged every believer to **examine himself** before partaking. We are to test our motives for coming to the Lord's Supper. Have we come without a high concern for others (1 Cor. 11:17-22)? Have we come without a proper regard for the Lord and His death (vv. 23-27)? It is better to stay away than to come wrongly and so to sin. On the other hand, such self-examination was not meant to forbid participation but rather to encourage right participation. Having tested oneself, one **should eat of the bread and drink of the cup.**

Verses 29-30: **For whoever eats and drinks without recognizing the body, eats and drinks judgment on himself. 30This is why many are sick and ill among you, and many have fallen asleep.**

Paul's teachings here bring up some important questions. Do some believers today become sick because of spiritual problems, such as partaking of the Lord's Supper unworthily? Do you think this has ever happened to you? Why? Does the Lord ever "call someone home to be with Him" as a disciplinary measure? How should you live as a result?

Paul believed that the Corinthians should be **recognizing the body** as they shared together in the Lord's Supper. In the context of 1 Corinthians, "body" might refer to two different things.

First, "body" might refer to *Christ's physical body*, represented in the bread of the Lord's Supper. That is, some of the Corinthians may not have realized that the bread they were partaking of was a sacred symbol. They were taking what Christ intended as a holy and solemn memorial of His crucifixion and were treating it as ordinary bread.

Second, "body" might refer to *the Corinthian congregation* as a local expression of the body of Christ (1 Cor. 12:13,27). In other words, some of the Corinthians may not have understood that their church was intended as a place of fellowship and unity rather than as a place to display a divisive spirit, with some members lording it over others.

In light of the warning that follows in verse 30, the second meaning seems more likely. The Lord's Supper should be a wonderful commemoration of Christian unity in Christ and with each other. This is the reason some churches use the term *communion* in reference to the Lord's Supper. Whenever someone partakes without recognizing this, he **eats and drinks judgment on himself.**

Paul was speaking of the Lord's disciplinary activity among believers so that they would not face final condemnation at the judgment. Among the Corinthians, the Lord's discipline had already taken two forms. First, some had become **sick and ill.** Second, others had died prematurely; they had **fallen asleep.** In the New Testament the phrase "fall asleep" is used either to refer to literal sleep or as a euphemism for the death of a righteous person. It is never used to refer to the death of the wicked or unbelieving (see John 11:11; Acts 7:60; 1 Cor. 15:6,18,20; 1 Thess. 4:13-15).

Notice that there is no place in Paul's teaching for finger pointing. No one comprehending Paul's words should ever begin to think, *I wonder if Mrs. Jones got cancer because the Lord was judging her.* The point, of course, is that believers are to examine themselves, not others, in this matter.

Verses 31-32: **If we were properly evaluating ourselves, we would not be judged, ³²but when we are judged, we are disciplined by the Lord, so that we may not be condemned with the world.**

Earlier Paul had said that Christians should **examine** themselves before coming to the Lord's table (v. 28). This verb suggests the idea of self-examination and passing the test as one approved. In verse 31 Paul used a different verb, translated **properly evaluating** oneself. This term suggests careful discernment of what is real and valuable. It is translated **recognizing** in verse 29. Thus, just as believers are to discern the body when they come to the Lord's table, so they are to discern themselves—their attitudes and actions. If they do this for themselves, they will **not be judged.**

Verse 32 makes clear the great difference between believers being **disciplined by the Lord** and people of **the world** ultimately being **condemned.** On the one hand, Christ's sacrificial death secures everlasting forgiveness for all those who believe, as Paul explained elsewhere: "No condemnation now exists for those in Christ Jesus" (Rom. 8:1). At the same time, as a loving Father, God disciplines His errant children: "He does it [discipline] for our benefit, so that we can share His holiness" (Heb. 12:10). On the other hand, unbelievers will one day face God's final judgment, resulting in their eternal condemnation and separation from Him (2 Thess. 1:8-9).

In His love, God sends situations into our lives so that we will make continuous progress in worship, maturity, and Christlike character. Whenever this happens, we should respond quickly with a spiritual self-evaluation. In this way we can approach the Lord's Supper full of confidence that we are truly proclaiming the Lord's death until He comes.

What lasting truths are in these verses?

1. Christians can participate in the Lord's Supper the wrong way.

2. Believers should examine themselves before they partake of the Lord's Supper.

3. Believers are especially to be aware of "the body" at the Lord's Supper.

4. God disciplines those who do not partake of the Lord's Supper the right way.

❖ *Spiritual Transformations*

The *Life Question* this lesson seeks to address is, What significance does the Lord's Supper have for me and for my church? The answer has come from an examination of two passages. When Jesus initiated the Lord's Supper, He told His disciples that the bread represented His body and the cup represented His blood. He told them that His death would establish the new covenant and that forgiveness of sins would be secured by His death. He promised that beyond death He would drink the cup with them again in the kingdom. Paul explained to the Corinthian believers that the Lord's Supper was to be observed on a regular basis. It has *past* meaning (in remembrance of Jesus); it has *present* meaning (as a proclamation of His death); it has a *future* meaning (looking forward to His return). Because of its great importance, the Lord's Supper should not be observed lightly. Church members are to examine themselves, lest they partake unworthily.

How would you now answer the Life Question for this study?
_____

Whom do you know that may be confused about the Lord's Supper and with whom you might share this message? _____

How do you personally prepare spiritually to observe the Lord's Supper? _____

Do you participate in the Lord's Supper "often"? If not, what should you do about it? If so, how often do you so commemorate the Lord's death? _____
_____

Prayer of Commitment: *Lord Jesus, Thank You for Your death for the forgiveness of sins and for giving us the Lord's Supper in remembrance of You. Help me always to examine myself so that I may partake of the Lord's Supper in a worthy manner. Amen.*

CHURCH LEADERSHIP

Background Passages: 1 Timothy 3:1-7; 5:17-18;Hebrews 13:7-9,17-18
Focal Passages: 1 Timothy 3:1-7; 5:17-18; Hebrews 13:7,17-18
Key Verse: Hebrews 13:17

❖ *Significance of the Lesson*

• The *Theme* of this lesson is that the church of Jesus Christ needs godly leaders who meet biblical qualifications, and believers have a responsibility to respect and support those leaders.

• The *Life Question* this lesson seeks to address is, Who can be church leaders and what is my responsibility toward these leaders?

• The *Biblical Truth* is that the church needs biblically qualified people in places of leadership. Leaders and non-leaders have mutual responsibilities to each other.

• The *Life Impact* is to help you support and submit to godly church leaders.

Why Study Church Leadership?

Trends of the last 50 years in American culture have challenged our ideas about authority and leadership. Those in authority have been ignored, criticized, and treated with contempt. Sometimes this kind of disrespect for leaders has crept into churches. Many churches have discarded leaders who have been faithful stewards of their responsibilities to lead in a godly manner.

Paul explained that leaders are essential in the life of a congregation. Such leaders, however, are to be biblically qualified to hold positions of authority in Christ's churches. The writer of Hebrews challenged his readers to obey and submit to the leaders in their midst.

Word Study: *Overseer* (1 Tim. 3:1)

In secular Greek the noun *episkopos* usually referred to community officials or leaders. In the New Testament, however, it is a title describing spiritually qualified leaders within a local congregation. It occurs five times in the New Testament (Acts 20:28; Phil. 1:1; 1 Tim. 3:2; Titus 1:7; 1 Pet. 2:25). The translation "bishop" perhaps suggests prestige and pomp to modern readers, an idea foreign to Scripture. Because New Testament overseers were humble servant-leaders, many contemporary versions translate *episkopos* with a word such as "overseer" or "guardian." All the biblical uses of the term are in Pauline settings except 1 Peter 2:25, in which Jesus is called "the shepherd and guardian of your souls." In the New Testament the term *episkopos* is used interchangeably with *presbuteros* ("elder"; see Acts 20:17,28; Titus 1:5,7).

❖ Search the Scriptures

As Paul neared the end of his ministry as a church planter and letter writer, he gave attention to the matter of how congregations should be led and organized. In his first letter to his associate Timothy, written around A.D. 63, he offered considerable advice about the need for properly qualified leaders in the churches. He also informed Timothy about the proper way for members to support these leaders.

A few years later, another Christian wrote a letter (Hebrews), this time to a congregation of Jewish Christians. The author instructed his readers about how to submit to and pray for their church leaders.

Qualifications for Leaders (1 Tim. 3:1-7)

*What does **aspires to be an overseer** mean? How can a church leader be **above reproach**? How could a church leader fall into the Devil's trap? What is the trap?*

Verse 1: This saying is trustworthy: "If anyone aspires to be an overseer, he desires a noble work."

Five times in his letters to Timothy and Titus, Paul reminded his young associates of certain key teachings by using the phrase, **This saying is trustworthy** (1 Tim. 1:15; 3:1; 4:9; 2 Tim. 2:11; Titus 3:8). These are the only places in the Bible such solemn affirmations are found. The matter of good church leaders was urgent for the Apostle Paul. People entrusted with the office of **overseer,** however, should be warned that it involves **work.** Such work is **noble** (or good), but there is no room for lazy people to lead a local church.

The Greek verb for **aspires** carries the idea of stretching out toward something in order to grasp it. The verb **desires** could be rendered "longs for." Because God is the One who calls people to church ministries, we should understand this as a God-given compulsion, not a selfish desire for power or prestige. Without an eager longing to serve, however, the work will become monotonous and the overseer will find his task only drudgery and duty.

***Verses 2-3:* An overseer, therefore, must be above reproach, the husband of one wife, self-controlled, sensible, respectable, hospitable, an able teacher, ³not addicted to wine, not a bully but gentle, not quarrelsome, not greedy.**

All who desire to lead are not necessarily spiritually qualified. Paul first listed a number of positive requirements and followed them with some negative ones. They all can be summarized by the first trait in the list: **above reproach** ("blameless," KJV), which is literally "not to be taken hold of." This does not mean sinless but indicates that there should be no matters in the leader's life that an outsider could point to and cause shame or blame to the church.

The first positive quality found in a blameless man is **the husband of one wife.** This phrase is literally "a one-woman man." The focus is on the positive characteristic of the overseer's faithfulness to his wife. Thus, someone with a history of marital infidelity would be disqualified. Paul also had a negative quality in mind. Bible interpreters have debated whether Paul was simply forbidding polygamy (having two or more wives at the same time) or also divorce and remarriage (having two or more wives but not at the same time). Many interpreters (including the present writer) favor the second view. Every church is responsible for choosing as leaders only those who have proven steadfast in marriage.

Two more qualities for an overseer are **self-controlled** and **sensible.** The ideas behind these words suggest a person with good sense and the ability to make wise decisions, first of all about oneself and one's family. Someone with good judgment in these areas will be likely to exercise proper discernment when it comes to leading the church.

An overseer must be **respectable** and **hospitable.** The first term includes the idea of a well-ordered life; the second suggests being at ease as a host. Persons whose lives are in disorder or who don't have any inclination to be sociable are unlikely to function well as church leaders.

Further, an overseer must also be **an able teacher.** This characteristic is the one area in which overseers' qualifications are different from deacons (see 1 Tim. 3:8-11). Deacons were helpers or assistants in the first century churches and therefore were not required to be preachers or teachers. Overseers, however, were entrusted with the task of teaching God's Word to members of the congregation.

Several negative qualifications for the overseer are given, starting with **not addicted to wine.** Use of alcohol is well associated with loss of good judgment. Church leaders therefore do well to refrain from every substance that could hinder their ability to lead God's people. This includes not only all forms of intoxicating beverages but also abuse of prescribed medications as well as illegal drugs.

An overseer must also be one who is **not a bully but gentle, not quarrelsome.** Today we are familiar with the phrase "good people skills." Those who are violent and contentious in their dealings with people are not likely to be able to help God's people grow toward Christian maturity. No church wants a leader known for arguing and fighting. The opposite is to be **gentle** or kind.

An overseer must avoid being **greedy.** This could also be translated "not a money lover." Those who make money their priority cannot have God or God's people as a priority. Unfortunately, many church leaders have demonstrated that they were in ministry for the money rather than for the love of God and His people (see Matt. 6:24).

Verses 4-5: **One who manages his own household competently, having his children under control with all dignity. [5](If anyone does not know how to manage his own household, how will he take care of God's church?)**

Just as a man's relationship with his wife indicates whether he might be a good church leader, so does his relationship with **his children.** Of course, there are no perfect children (or perfect parents) and a leader's children must be allowed to be children. Yet some fathers are too lax; some are too strict. There is a balance, and the one who **manages . . . competently** can be recognized by the way his children act. Are they **under control with all dignity**? The term **dignity** could refer to the fathers or to the children. Because little children cannot be expected to be dignified and adult children are no longer under the control of the father, it may be best to apply this term to the fathers.

Verse 5 is Paul's logical deduction. **God's church** is like a big family. Thus, the same qualities involved in a man's guidance of **his own household** will be effective when it comes to his leadership over the family of God. The verb translated **manage** could be translated "stand over" in the sense of supervise. This is not, however, the rule of a dictator but the loving care of a nurse, as the verb **take care of** shows (used elsewhere only in Luke 10:34-35). All who lead in God's church soon discover that there is a great deal of caring for those who have been spiritually and emotionally wounded. Without a heart for taking care of people's needs—demonstrated by lovingly caring for his own children—an overseer is doomed to failure.

Verses 6-7: **He must not be a new convert, or he might become conceited and fall into the condemnation of the Devil. ⁷Furthermore, he must have a good reputation among outsiders, so that he does not fall into disgrace and the Devil's trap.**

All the qualifications Paul had listed so far imply that a church leader has had time to mature in his faith before he is given responsibility over a congregation. Now Paul made the point explicit. An overseer **must not be a new convert.** Paul supported this with an excellent reason. Those who are promoted into church leadership too quickly are tempted to become **conceited.** Leadership can cause people to become puffed up so that they think themselves greater than they really are (see Prov. 16:18).

Two main interpretations have been suggested for the words **the condemnation of the Devil.** On the one hand, pride was probably the cause of the Devil's original rebellion against God that caused him to become condemned. Thus, the church leader who becomes conceited might try to lead without looking humbly to God for direction—and thus become like the Devil. On the other hand, the Devil may use the pride he finds within a church leader to lure a man into sin and a fall. For example, conceit joined with sexual desire or greed has caused the downfall of many church leaders.

Not only must those inside the church know that their leaders have been truly converted, but **among outsiders** (unbelievers) a man **must have a good reputation.** Church leaders are generally a congregation's "face" to the public. A congregation must therefore choose carefully those who will represent them. Church leaders who become known as loose in their morals, poor money managers, or without integrity in their speech can only lead to ridicule for the congregation. Even the unbelieving world holds church leaders to a higher standard than it does other people. Whenever a church leader falls publicly, he falls **into disgrace** and shame, and his congregation could get a black eye as well.

To all believers the Apostle Peter warned, "Your adversary the Devil is prowling around like a roaring lion, looking for anyone he can devour" (1 Pet. 5:8). Because this is true for all believers, how much truer is it for church leaders that a **Devil's trap** is waiting to catch them? Those who have been following Christ long enough to become mature and have been tested and found to be "above reproach" (1 Tlm. 3:2) will be able to draw on the strength of the Lord to avoid such a fate. Thus, the members of a local church have a grave responsibility to choose their leaders with great care, for such men are certainly going to be considered fair game for the Devil. Only by God's grace can Christians—whether leaders or followers—hope to succeed against the enemy.

What lasting truths are in these verses?

1. Not every believer is qualified to be a church leader.

2. Those who lead in a congregation should earnestly desire to do this work.

3. A potential leader should be tested and found to be above reproach before being put into leadership.

4. Every church leader is required to be faithful in marriage and careful in child rearing.

Support for Leaders (1 Tim. 5:17-18)

Is it biblical to provide financial support for church leaders? How should the effectiveness of such leaders be measured?

Verse 17: The elders who are good leaders should be considered worthy of an ample honorarium, especially those who work hard at preaching and teaching.

Those who served as overseers in first-century churches were also called **elders.** Here Paul was giving instructions about those who had already met the qualifications he had outlined in 1 Timothy 3:1-7. These men were therefore already active. What were they doing? First, they were working at being **good leaders.** This translates the same Greek verb as "manages" in 1 Timothy 3:4. Just as every Christian father is to manage his family well, so elders are to lead well.

Second, Paul stated that such elders were to **work hard at preaching and teaching.** The words **at preaching and teaching** are literally "in word and in teaching." This shows that at the heart of leading a congregation is preaching the Word of God. Unless a church is being fed the nourishment of the Scriptures, it will not grow—no matter how well it is otherwise being led. Paul was aware that this was no easy task; it is hard work. This text is one of many that shows why Baptists—and many other Christian groups—have insisted that the Bible-based sermon must remain central when the church is gathered for worship.

Effective overseers have a demanding task. They must manage the church. They must work hard at teaching God's Word. The church must therefore give them an **ample honorarium.** The original Greek is literally "double honor" (KJV) and means that better work should mean better pay! In the first century it was probably unheard of for a church to be able to afford a full-time pastor. Even then, however, church members were to recognize that their leaders had financial needs to meet. People must not consider church leadership as a way to get rich, but churches should honor good leaders monetarily.

Verse 18: **For the Scripture says: You must not muzzle an ox that is threshing grain, and, The laborer is worthy of his wages.**

Paul gave two illustrations to support the idea that those who work hard should be adequately compensated. He took both examples from **Scripture.** First, he quoted Deuteronomy 25:4. Under the law of Moses, an ox that would thresh grain was permitted to eat some of the grain it had helped produce. If God mercifully cared for the needs of working livestock, how much more does He care for the material needs of working church leaders! Paul quoted this same verse in 1 Corinthians 9:9 where he made a similar point about financial compensation for those whose labor is in the gospel (see also v. 14).

Paul's second illustration is from the teachings of Jesus. **The laborer is worthy of his wages** is an exact quote of Luke 10:7, when Jesus sent out the 70 preachers in pairs. Paul quoted Deuteronomy and Jesus here and referred to them both as **Scripture.** This shows how highly the teachings of Jesus were regarded in the early church. It is also possible that Paul already had a copy of Luke's Gospel by this time and was therefore quoting the Gospel of Luke as Scripture. But he may have learned about Jesus' statement from another source.

What lasting truths are in these verses?

1. Church leaders are to work hard not only at managing the people but also at ministering the Word.

2. One way that congregations are responsible to esteem their leaders is by providing them with good pay.

3. Both Testaments teach that God's will is for diligent workers to have their material needs met.

Follow Leaders' Examples (Heb. 13:7)

*How can a church **remember** its leaders? In what ways should church members **imitate** their leaders?*

Verse 7: Remember your leaders who have spoken God's word to you. As you carefully observe the outcome of their lives, imitate their faith.

As the author of Hebrews was closing his letter, he had a few more instructions to leave with his readers. One of these was to **remember your leaders.** The term **leaders** is more general than "overseer" or "elder," which were official titles in New Testament churches. The wording of the verse suggests that some of these leaders may have died. Remembering those who have successfully completed the race of the Christian life can provide great encouragement.

The service of these leaders was twofold. First, they had **spoken God's word** (see 1 Tim. 5:17). Second, they lived lives so open to inspection that believers could **carefully observe** them. In other words, they had led by example as well as by instruction. The term **lives** renders a Greek noun that could also be translated "lifestyles." Here is an indirect reminder of 1 Timothy 3:1-7. The character traits of those chosen as church leaders matter a great deal because they are a model for other believers. All Christians—not just leaders—should seek to live above reproach. Here the quality of **faith** is especially to be modeled by leaders so that ordinary believers can grow in their faith as well. Earlier the writer had given a similar instruction, asking the readers to become "imitators of those who inherit the promises through faith and perseverance" (Heb. 6:12).

There is a threefold charge to the members: **remember . . . observe . . . imitate.** Thus, one measure of whether a church has godly leaders is whether those who are following them have grown in their ability to trust God. Not only are members responsible to choose qualified leaders, but they are to seek to conform to the living examples set by these godly leaders.

What lasting truths are in this verse?

1. The most important way that church leaders lead is by speaking God's Word.

2. Believers are responsible to remember and observe the good examples of their leaders' faith so that they can mirror that faith in their own lives.

Submit to and Pray for Leaders (Heb. 13:17-18)

*Why should believers submit to church leaders? Why did the writer use such strong emotional words—**joy** and **grief**—in speaking about submitting to leaders? How should members pray for their leaders?*

Verse 17: Obey your leaders and submit to them, for they keep watch over your souls as those who will give an account, so that they can do this with joy and not with grief, for that would be unprofitable for you.

American Christians sometimes have a difficult time understanding why they should **obey** and **submit to** those who are their **leaders.** The Greek verbs do not, however, imply the blind obedience or the unquestioning submission implied at first glance. The verb **obey** carries with it the idea of "being persuaded" toward the right course of belief or action. The verb **submit** ("do what they say," NLT, CEV) includes the notion of yielding to those who lead.

Christian leaders have a great shepherding responsibility for their spiritual sheep. They are constantly to **keep watch over** their **souls,** knowing that their enemies—the world, the flesh and the Devil—come against God's people. The reference to "various kinds of strange teachings" in verse 9 indicates that the original readers were in danger of being led astray by false doctrines. Spiritual leaders will **give an account** to God when they face His judgment for how well they carried out their God-given task of protecting their people (1 Cor. 3:10-15; 2 Cor. 5:10).

When members resist their spiritual leaders, the end result for the leaders is **grief**—groaning because they recognize that their sheep have endangered themselves. When leaders experience this, they may lose heart and find their work too much drudgery. When leaders are weighed down because of the contentiousness of the congregation, it becomes **unprofitable** to the people. Instead, the people should so willingly respond to their leaders that it brings **joy** to the leaders' hearts. I once knew a pastor who ended every column in the church's monthly newsletter with the words, "It is a joy to be your pastor." It is no surprise that he had a long and effective pastorate in that church.

Verse 18: Pray for us; for we are convinced that we have a clear conscience, wanting to conduct ourselves honorably in everything.

As a church leader himself, the author asked that the readers **pray for** him. All church leaders long to know that many of the members are praying regularly for them. This passage suggests two kinds of things for which members can pray for their leaders. First, they should pray that their leaders would maintain **a clear conscience,** not falling into any temptation to sin. Second, they should pray for their leaders to **conduct** themselves **honorably in everything.** This speaks of the need for an ongoing lifestyle that is above reproach. Every church leader longs to hear the final approval from the Lord: "Well done, good and faithful slave! You were faithful over a few things. I will put you in charge of many things. Enter your master's joy!" (Matt. 25:23).

What lasting truths are in these verses?

1. Church members are responsible to God for yielding to godly leaders.

2. Church members should pray regularly for their spiritual leaders.

3. Church leaders are accountable to God for the way they lead.

4. Church leaders have a right to find joy in their spiritual ministries.

❖ *Spiritual Transformations*

The *Life Question* this lesson seeks to address is, Who can be church leaders and what is my responsibility toward these leaders? The answer has come from studying parts of two letters. When Paul wrote to Timothy, he instructed him that only those with certain spiritual qualities should become overseers or elders. He further noted that those who carry out effective work in teaching the Word and tending to the church should be supported financially. The writer to the Hebrews used a number of strong verbs to describe the relationship of Christian people to their leaders: *remember, observe, imitate, obey, submit,* and *pray for.* At the same time, he taught that leaders are accountable to guide God's people carefully, looking for joy both in this life as well as in eternity.

How would you characterize your relationship with the spiritual leaders in your congregation? Is there an attitude you should change or an action you should take? What is it? _____

_____

Consider writing one of the leaders in your church, expressing your support and your commitment to regular prayer on his behalf.

Prayer of Commitment: *Lord Jesus, Thank You for providing godly leaders for Your churches throughout the centuries. Thank You for the leaders You have placed over me in my local congregation. Help me to support them, follow their example, and pray for them. Amen.*

SPIRITUAL GIFTS

Background Passage: 1 Corinthians 12:1-30
Focal Passages: 1 Corinthians 12:4-15,20,27
Key Verses: 1 Corinthians 12:12-14

❖ *Significance of the Lesson*

• The *Theme* of this lesson is that the Holy Spirit empowers all believers with spiritual gifts that they should use to glorify God and edify His people.

• The *Life Question* this lesson seeks to address is, What is the purpose of spiritual gifts and how can I use mine in a way that pleases God?

• The *Biblical Truth* is that spiritual gifts are to build up the body of Christ, the church, not to build up the individual exercising the gift.

• The *Life Impact* is to help you discover and exercise your spiritual gifts.

Why Study Spiritual Gifts?

The topic of spiritual gifts is subject to extremes. On the one hand, many believers ignore their gifts or are not interested in using their gifts in their church. Others do not even know that they have spiritual gifts. On the other hand, some Christian circles overstress—or even abuse—certain spiritual gifts. Either extreme reflects poorly on Jesus Christ, the founder and head of the church. The Lord wants every church to be balanced concerning spiritual gifts, yet this happens only as a congregation seeks to understand and follow the teachings of Scripture on this important subject.

The Apostle Paul is the best source of biblical guidance on spiritual gifts. He directed the Christians in Corinth to exercise their spiritual gifts in a way that would build up the entire body of Christ, the church. He asked them to recognize that all members of the body were of equal importance to God and to use their gifts for the benefit of others, not for themselves.

Word Study: *Spirit* (1 Cor. 12:4)

In Greek the noun *pneuma* is derived from the verb *pneo*, "to blow." Thus, "wind" or "breath" is the meaning in a few contexts. In the New Testament, however, *pneuma* usually means "spirit" as a reference to that which is nonmaterial in living beings, whether natural or supernatural. Thus, "spirit" is a quality attributed variously to angels, demons, and humans (Matt. 8:16; Rom. 1:9; Heb. 1:14).

About 240 of the 379 instances of *pneuma* in the New Testament refer to the Spirit of God, or the Holy Spirit. In Christian teaching, the Holy Spirit is the third Person of the Trinity, equal in eternality, power, and glory with the Father and the Son (see Matt. 28:19). Three New Testament writers emphasized the Holy Spirit's person and work: Luke, John, and Paul. Jesus promised that the Holy Spirit would baptize believers, and this was first fulfilled on the day of Pentecost (Acts 1:4-5; 2:1-4). The dwelling of the Holy Spirit in believers is what marks them as belonging to Christ (Rom. 8:9). Paul taught extensively about the gifts of the Spirit to individual believers in 1 Corinthians 12–14.

❖ *Search the Scriptures*

Paul wrote 1 Corinthians about A.D. 55. He sent it to the thriving congregation he had founded in Corinth about five years earlier during his second missionary journey. Paul had learned about a number of difficulties that were disrupting this church. His letter was written from a pastoral heart full of love and concern for them.

One reason Paul wrote was to correct problems associated with the exercise of spiritual gifts, which he addressed in chapters 12–14. He emphasized that the Holy Spirit has given spiritual gifts to all believers for the good of all the other members of Christ's body. He taught that there is both unity and diversity in the gifts of the Spirit. He further taught that, just as with the human body, no member of the body of Christ is more important than another is.

Purpose of Gifts (1 Cor. 12:4-7)

*What did Paul mean by **gifts**? Is there a distinction between gifts, ministries, and activities? How did Paul's understanding of the Godhead as Trinity affect his understanding of spiritual gifts?*

Verses 4-7: **Now there are different gifts, but the same Spirit. ⁵There are different ministries, but the same Lord. ⁶And there are different activities, but the same God is active in everyone and everything. ⁷A manifestation of the Spirit is given to each person to produce what is beneficial.**

Paul was writing to members of the church in Corinth, so when he spoke about **each person,** he was referring to all those in the congregation, not to unbelievers. His topic was spiritual **gifts.** The Greek term is *charismata* (plural; the singular is *charisma*, the source for the our word *charismatic*). It was derived from the noun *charis*, meaning "grace." **Gifts,** as Paul taught about them here, refers to abilities given to **each person** in the body of Christ because of God's grace. There is nothing a believer can do to earn a spiritual gift—any more than one can earn salvation. God bestows spiritual **gifts** to all who have been born again, just as surely as He distributes natural talents to all human beings who have ever been born.

In order to shed further light on the meaning of **gifts,** Paul used three additional terms in this passage. Each of them focuses on a slightly different aspect of the same truth, just as shining three different spotlights on a skyscraper at night reveals distinct aspects of the same building.

First, the term **ministries** carries the idea of helping or serving others. It is closely related to "deacon," which originally referred to someone who served tables. Second, the term **activities** suggests the energy that it takes to **produce what is beneficial.** God accomplishes **everything** regarding spiritual gifts in **everyone** in the body of Christ. Building up other believers does not happen accidentally but deliberately. Using spiritual gifts is not passive but active, and Christians are to be intentional about developing and using their spiritual gifts. Third, the word **manifestation** includes the idea of showing forth. The Holy Spirit gives His gifts to reveal His presence and power in the life of a believer so that others will benefit. Christians are not to hide their gifts but to use them openly. This is not a matter of believers parading self but rather showing how **the Spirit,** who has bestowed these gifts, works in their lives.

In verses 4-6 Paul used a triple repetition of two separate terms: **different . . . different . . . different,** and **same . . . same . . . same.** He could hardly have emphasized the idea of diversity in unity more clearly. **Different** means "a variety of" or "various kinds of." Think about how human beings come in different shapes, sizes, and colors.

Consider how natural talents come in so many varieties—music, mathematics, athletics. The term **same** emphasizes the sole source of spiritual gifts: there is only one Triune God, and He is the only giver of gifts (see also Eph. 4:4-6).

Paul's careful wording in this passage demonstrates his understanding of God as existing in three Persons. Christians are accustomed to thinking of the order Father, Son, Spirit; here Paul reversed the order, perhaps because the order was not yet "set" in the writings of Christians: **Spirit . . . Lord . . . God.** The **Spirit** is certainly the Holy Spirit, not the human spirit. The **Lord** refers to Jesus, as the close parallel to verse 3 shows. **God** refers to the Heavenly Father.

In summary, Paul was saying that the *one* God (Father-Son-Spirit) has given *many* gifts (ministries-activities-manifestations) to His people. What is His purpose? God's intent is **to produce what is beneficial.** Gifts aren't assigned in order to build up the recipient of the gift. They are for the good of the whole, to be used for everyone's advantage. When spiritual gifts are used only to the advantage of the recipient, they are being abused.

What lasting truths are in these verses?

1. All spiritual gifts come from God alone: Father, Son, and Spirit.
2. God has given spiritual gifts to every believer.
3. Spiritual gifts are to be manifested in ministry and activity so that other believers will benefit.

Diversity of Gifts (1 Cor. 12:8-10)

Was Paul making an official list of spiritual gifts in this passage? To what degree can we be sure about what activities Paul was describing in this text?

Verses 8-10: To one is given a message of wisdom through the Spirit, to another, a message of knowledge by the same Spirit, [9]to another, faith by the same Spirit, to another, gifts of healing by the one Spirit, [10]to another, the performing of miracles, to another, prophecy, to another, distinguishing between spirits, to another, different kinds of languages, to another, interpretation of languages.

Surely Paul would have been surprised to learn how controversial these verses have become. The Corinthians surely understood exactly what he was talking about. Today's Bible students struggle to grasp Paul's meaning. A few things are abundantly clear. First, this is simply a representative list of nine gifts among many others. Romans 12:6-8 has another list that has some similarities and some differences with this one. Paul would probably no more have had an official list in mind than we could have an official inventory of natural talents—even though we all could list any number of talents.

Second, Paul emphasized the single divine source of all gifts (1 Cor. 12:4-7). Note the many ways he said this: **through the Spirit . . . by the same Spirit . . . by the one Spirit.** In these verses Paul emphasized the Spirit, but what he had said earlier about the Father and about the Lord Jesus as the originator of gifts is still assumed.

Third, when listing these gifts, Paul often used plural forms, as if to underscore that diversity is present even within a single kind of gift: **gifts of healing . . . miracles . . . different kinds of languages.** As an analogy, there are many kinds of musical talent—vocal, instrumental, compositional—as well as various kinds of athletic talent—speed, strength, agility.

Fourth, these gifts can be divided into two groups. Some gifts focus on what believers are enabled to *say;* others focus on how believers *serve* (see 1 Pet. 4:11 for this grouping). In the discussion that follows, note whether the focus is on *speech* or *service.* Consider the believers you know in your congregation. Most can readily be identified as "speakers" or "servers" in their church ministries.

The correct understanding of the nature of these gifts has been the subject of many debates, sermons, and books. This study cannot hope to solve all the problems that may arise, but we need to consider what Paul meant by these nine gifts.

1. **Message of wisdom.** Wisdom (*sophia* in Greek) has been called the application of knowledge in a given situation. God has given some people the ability to put facts together clearly and carefully so that wise decisions can be made by a church or by an individual church member. I once served on a church committee that easily reached a united decision about calling a new staff member immediately after the committee chairman thoughtfully reviewed for us all the facts about the various candidates. This man likely had the gift of wisdom.

2. **Message of knowledge.** The word **knowledge** here has to do with gaining new information or understanding. For example, what I am doing right now as the writer of this Bible study material is passing on my insight about the meaning of a certain Bible passage. Skilled Sunday School teachers are exercising the **message of knowledge** to

those in their classes, even though they may not have called their gift by this name.

3. **Faith** is here not the faith that saves, because every Christian possesses faith as a gift of God (Eph. 2:8-9). Rather, Paul meant a particularly strong God-given ability to determine the will of God and then to trust Him to bring it to pass. In turn, this will build up other believers. Missionaries and church planters—those who risk moving to new places and doing what has never been done before—are often trailblazers for others who will succeed them. Many Christian hospitals, colleges, seminaries, orphanages, and a thousand other endeavors are flourishing today because certain believers used their God-given faith. Others followed their faith, and God's kingdom has benefited as a result.

4. **Gifts of healing** is plural, as if Paul were saying that God brings about many different kinds of healing—not only physical but also spiritual and emotional. It should also be noted that Paul emphasized divine *healing* rather than divine *healers.* Surely at times God does heal using miraculous means (see Jas. 5:14-15). Sometimes He uses medicine and natural means. Sometimes He does not heal (see 2 Tim. 4:20). Every time Christians pray for a loved one or friend to be healed from sickness, they are affirming that they believe God is ultimately the One who heals.

5. **Miracles** in the Book of Acts often became occasions that led to proclaiming the gospel of Christ (see Acts 3). In the four Gospels, Jesus refused to do miracles just for the sake of doing miracles (as in Luke 11:29). We can be sure that when God's glory and goodness are best shown through miracles, He will see that they occur, even today. Many missionaries, especially in areas where the gospel is going for the first time, have reported extraordinary events that are indeed miraculous. These events have led thousands of lost people to faith in Christ.

6. **Prophecy** refers to speaking forth God's words. The biblical prophets did not focus primarily on predicting the future (although the Bible contains many such prophecies). It is best to think about prophecy in two distinct senses. First, the biblical prophets were men inspired by the Holy Spirit who recorded revelations from God so that these revelations are now in Scripture. In this sense the church is "built on the foundation of the apostles and prophets, with Christ Jesus Himself as the cornerstone" (Eph. 2:20). There are no more prophets

like this, because "the faith . . . was delivered to the saints once for all" (Jude 3). The Scriptural revelation of God is complete, and there will be no more inspired prophets to add to Scripture (see Heb. 1:1-3).

Second, there are gifted individuals today whose ministry is to speak forth God's Word, those who have a powerful ability to say "thus saith the Lord." The long ministry of Billy Graham readily comes to mind. Many local church leaders—as well as other believers—function with prophetic clarity in proclaiming God's Word.

7. **Distinguishing between spirits** probably had do with recognizing whether an evil spirit was working in someone's life (see 1 Cor. 12:2-3). The idolatry out of which many of the Corinthian Christians had been delivered was not benign but evil, often empowered by demonic forces. Satan "is disguised as an angel of light" (2 Cor. 11:14); therefore, God has given some believers special insight to recognize where satanic power is at work so that others will not be tricked. All believers, however, are to seek to learn scriptural teachings well enough to take their stand against the enemy (Eph. 6:10-17).

8. **Different kinds of languages** (the plural is used again) may refer to several different kinds of speech activities. On the day of Pentecost 120 believers were suddenly able to speak to foreigners in languages that they had never learned—and three thousand were converted to Christ (Acts 2). In the Corinthian church, evidently there were manifestations of speech that could not be understood by anyone present (1 Cor. 14:2; see also 13:1, "the languages of men and of angels"). Paul's feelings about this were clear: "I would rather speak five words with my understanding, in order to teach others also, than ten thousand words in another language" (14:19).

9. **Interpretation of languages** refers to the ability to translate in the church's public worship the speech of those who could not be understood by anyone present. Paul gave further instructions about this gift in 1 Corinthians 14:13-32. Some Christian groups today have ignored Paul's teaching, particularly verses 27-28: "If any person speaks in another language, there should be only two, or at the most three, each in turn, and someone must interpret. But if there is no interpreter, that person should keep silent in the church."

What lasting truths are in these verses?

1. This passage contains a representative list of spiritual gifts.

2. Some spiritual gifts focus on activities of speech, such as wisdom, knowledge, prophecy, languages, and interpretation.

3. Some spiritual gifts focus on activities of service, such as faith, healings, miracles, and distinguishing between spirits.

Unity of Gifts (1 Cor. 12:11-15,20,27)

*What did Paul mean by **baptized by one Spirit**? Why did Paul use the human body to illustrate the proper use of spiritual gifts?*

Verses 11-13: But one and the same Spirit is active in all these, distributing to each one as He wills. [12]For as the body is one and has many parts, and all the parts of that body, though many, are one body—so also is Christ. [13]For we were all baptized by one Spirit into one body—whether Jews or Greeks, whether slaves or free—and we were all made to drink of one Spirit.

Paul had taught the Corinthians that the purpose of spiritual gifts is to benefit the whole congregation. He had emphasized that these gifts come in many varieties. In verses 11-15 he developed a theme he had already noted in verses 4-7: the unity of gifts. Paul gave four reasons that gifts are a unity. First, the gifts come from **one and the same Spirit.** It is only as **He wills** that **each one** has been assigned gifts. Second, they work together in **one body,** the local fellowship of believers.

In verse 12 Paul began developing the parallel between a human body and the congregation as a body. In both cases **the body is one.** In both cases it **has many parts.** There is unity without uniformity. Note the end of verse 12. We might have expected Paul to say, "so also is the church," but instead he said, **so also is Christ.** Paul can say this because Christ is "the head of the body, the church" (Col. 1:18). Wherever Christ's body is, He is there as well. Christ's reputation therefore is "on the line" in the way a church exercises the gifts He has given them.

Third, gifts are a unity because **we were all baptized by one Spirit into one body.** One shared experience of all first-century believers was *visible* baptism by water (see the comments on Acts 2:38 in the lesson for the week of June 6). Similarly, a shared experience of all believers was *invisible* baptism by the Spirit **into one body,** that is, identification with the one body of Christ. This experience is an established fact for all believers (see Rom. 8:9), not something believers are to seek.

Fourth, gifts are a unity because all Christians have been **made to drink of one Spirit.** Paul used the analogy of a common well for all to use (see John 7:38-39). He also reminded the Corinthians of the various backgrounds they came from, both ethnic **(Jews or Greeks)** and socio-economic **(slaves or free).** Such distinctions among the members existed, but they were no longer a barrier to being **one body.**

Verses 14-15: **So the body is not one part but many. [15]If the foot should say, "Because I'm not a hand, I don't belong to the body," in spite of this it still belongs to the body.**

Here Paul began an extended analogy comparing the human as a body and the church as a body. This analogy goes all the way through verse 26. The essential truth is stated in verse 14. A church should remember that—like a human body—there **is not one part but many.** Many vital organs and many different limbs and other body parts all work together for the good of the whole body.

Paul's point in verses 15-16 is unmistakable. Body parts all belong to the body; no matter how much they want to be separate they belong together. Thus, in the body of Christ there is no room for either jealousy or rejection of differently gifted individuals. If one gifted with faith should say, "Because I'm not a prophet, I don't belong to the Christian body," that wouldn't change anything. **In spite of this,** such a person **still belongs to the body.**

Verse 20: **Now there are many parts, yet one body.**

The church as a whole can never be made up of persons all with the same gift. If all have speaking gifts, how would there be serving? If all had the special gift of faith, where would the message of wisdom be? There is great diversity—**many parts**—in the church, and this should be celebrated as God's will, for He "has placed the parts, each one of them, in the body just as He wanted" (v. 18). There is also great unity—**one body**—and this too is to be celebrated as the will of God.

Verse 27: **Now you are the body of Christ, and individual members of it.**

Every local church fellowship is called on to remember that Christ is the head of its fellowship. Collectively the saints of the Corinthian congregation made up **the body of Christ.** The individuals had not lost their distinctiveness, however, for all believers were to remember that they were **individual members of it.** Just as the hands, heart, feet, legs, and so on were still recognizable—and worked together for the benefit of the whole—so it is in the fellowship of Christ's church.

What lasting truths are in these verses?

1. Although persons do not lose their individuality in the body of Christ, they are always to remember that they belong together as part of the same body.

2. Because the one Holy Spirit is the source of all gifts, He bestows them according to His will.

3. The human body—with all its diverse parts—illustrates well that there is one body of Christ with many diverse members.

4. This diversity is to include not only persons with a variety of gifts but also persons from diverse ethnic and socio-economic backgrounds.

❖ *Spiritual Transformations*

The *Life Question* this lesson seeks to address is, What is the purpose of spiritual gifts and how can I use mine in a way that pleases God? The answer has come from studying 1 Corinthians 12. When Paul wrote to the church in Corinth, he told them that God has given spiritual gifts for the benefit of the entire congregation, not to build up the individual alone. His emphasis was balanced between showing the diversity of gifts and the unity of gifts.

Which of the lasting truths in this lesson speaks most to you?

_____

_____

Do you know someone who may have unscriptural ideas about spiritual gifts and with whom you could share this message? What do you think you need to say to this person? _____

_____

Check each of the following that applies to you:
___ *1. I have identified my spiritual gift(s).*
___ *2. I am regularly using my spiritual gift(s) in my local church.*
___ *3. I am grateful that God has given me the gift(s) that He has.*
___ *4. I work to uphold the unity of the body of Christ of which I am a member.*

If you are not able to check one or more of these statements, consider the course of action that you should take to change the situation and then do it.

Prayer of Commitment: *Lord Jesus, Thank You for the great variety of spiritual gifts that the Holy Spirit bestows. Thank You for the gifts that He has given me. Help me use them in such a way that the members of my church will benefit. Thank You for placing me as a part of a local church fellowship. Help me appreciate and support the unity of Your body. Amen.*

That's Encouraging!

Who or what encourages you? compliments from friends? reading a new devotional book? worshiping God on Sunday morning? Everyone benefits from encouragement, although some people seem to need it more than others do.

Many Christian young adults have made wonderful choices about education, career, and marriage. They can benefit by being encouraged to continue for the long haul—being faithful to Christ, their churches, and their families. Others may face discouragement. They know they have already made major mistakes. How can they be encouraged to serve Christ again?

Then there are those thousands in the middle of life. Children and careers are growing. Marriages are strong. They have a healthy relationship with Christ and His church. But what about others who have experienced failure? What happens when dreams and enthusiasm die? What happens when despair threatens to overwhelm?

Finally, there are the growing number of aging Baby Boomers and the generation older than that. Many face an empty nest, retirement, death of a spouse, or loss of health. These people do not have to give in to the feeling that life is over, that they are just waiting to die. What kind of encouragement does Scripture have for people like this?

No matter where you are in life's journey, you can find God's Word to be your greatest source of encouragement. You do not have to endure the "same old, same old." The studies for this month focus on four encouraging truths from Scripture. First, we will study God's enduring love and the confidence it brings us (July 4). The sure salvation that we have in Christ will be the second focus (July 11). The third study will draw our attention to encouragement through being useful servants of God (July 18). Finally, we will consider how to live with hope in God (July 25). Begin to pray now that God will use these studies to revitalize you. Be encouraged!

ENCOURAGED BY ENDURING LOVE

Bible Passages: Lamentations 3:19-24; Luke 19:1-10
Key Verse: Lamentations 3:22

❖ *Significance of the Lesson*

• The *Theme* of this lesson is that we can be encouraged in knowing that God loves us, regardless of who we are or what we've done.
• The *Life Question* this lesson seeks to address is, Why should I believe God loves me?
• The *Biblical Truth* is that God's love endures eternally and includes everyone.
• The *Life Impact* is to help you live in the confident assurance of God's love.

Is God's Love Real?

"Why should I believe in the love of God? I've never felt Him. Maybe it's just your imagination." Many people struggle with the concept of God's love. Some don't accept it because they don't believe there is a God. Others believe that He exists, but they perceive Him as cold or distant. They think of God as demanding or indifferent. Other people have a hard time believing that God's love is real because of all the evil and tragedies in the world. Still others accept the general idea of a loving God, but they think they are so sinful that God would never love them.

Scripture teaches that God's love is real despite circumstances, either internal or external. An Old Testament poem and an incident from the life of Jesus can serve as anchors for us to stake our lives on the truth that God's "love does not cease."

Word Study: *Faithful love* (Lam. 3:22)

The Hebrew noun *chesed* occurs nearly 250 times in the Old Testament. This term is quite rich and very difficult to translate. *Chesed* includes elements of love, mercy, steadfastness, and loyalty.

As an attribute of God, *chesed* was the basis of His reaching out to undeserving Israelites and establishing His covenants with them. God's *chesed* can be seen in that He continued to reach out in faithful love to Israel even when they deliberately rejected Him. God asked that His people return faithful love to Him, particularly in the Book of Hosea (6:6; 12:6). In the New Testament, mercy *(eleos)* and grace *(charis)* are the closest Greek counterparts to *chesed*.

The defining passage for *chesed* focuses on the Lord's (Yahweh's) revelation of Himself to Moses: "Yahweh—Yahweh is a compassionate and gracious God, slow to anger and rich in faithful love *[chesed]* and truth, maintaining faithful love *[chesed]* to a thousand generations, forgiving wrongdoing, rebellion, and sin" (Ex. 34:6-7).

❖ *Search the Scriptures*

In the year 586 B.C. the city of Jerusalem fell to the might of the Babylonian Empire. Solomon's temple was burned. The people of Judah were taken captive as slaves. Many asked if God's love had failed. Out of this bitter experience Jeremiah wrote the poems of Lamentations. In the midst of his grief and despair, he affirmed that God's faithful love offered encouragement for the future.

Over six centuries later, a sinful Jewish tax collector encountered the faithful love of God on a day and in a way he was not expecting. Jesus reached out to him and brought salvation both to him and to his household. Zacchaeus learned that God can and does reach out in love to individuals regardless of who they are or what they have done.

God's Love Never Ceases (Lam. 3:19-24)

Why was the writer of Lamentations so depressed? What remedy did he discover? What positive terms did he use to describe God's love for him? How can a poem written so long ago encourage people in today's world?

Verses 19-21: Remember my affliction and my homelessness, the wormwood and the poison.
20 I continually remember ⌊ them ⌋
  and have become depressed.
21 Yet I call this to mind,
  and therefore I have hope.

Lamentations 3:1-18 is one of the most anguish-filled passages in the entire Bible. These verses were carefully composed as the first part of an alphabetical poem (acrostic), in which the first line of each successive stanza begins with the next letter of the Hebrew alphabet. It's as if the writer were saying, "I am in grief from A to Z: anguished and agonized, bruised and broken, crying and crushed, distressed and distraught, empty and exiled, fearful and forlorn . . ." Verses 19-24 cover the letters *zayin* and *cheth,* the seventh and eighth letters of the Hebrew alphabet. The rest of Lamentations 3 covers the rest of the alphabet. (See the subheadings for Ps. 119, another alphabetical or acrostic poem, for all the Hebrew letters.)

Verses 19-21 each begin with *zayin.* Verse 19 reviews and summarizes the writer's experiences already mentioned in verses 1-18. His sorrow reflected the despair of everyone in the kingdom of Judah. He was full of **affliction,** as were thousands of others. He had experienced **homelessness,** being removed from his familiar environment. If the author was indeed Jeremiah, then Jeremiah 37–38 sheds a great deal of light on why he called his situation **the wormwood and the poison** ("wormwood and gall," KJV; a reference to plants that were bitter or poisonous).

The poet understood that God knew everything going on in his life. For him to be **depressed** ("bowed down within me," NASB) suggests that he was bearing a load that he felt was too heavy.

Life is that way sometimes. We may become distraught because of circumstances beyond our control, and all too often we are weighed down as a result of evil choices we have made. All of this means, however, that for us to recognize that we have been through (or are in the midst of) loss or grief or discouragement is not necessarily bad. Sometimes we are not ready to be encouraged until we admit that we are discouraged!

In the back of the inspired poet's **mind** there was a reason to **have hope** ready to burst forth. It had been there all along lying dormant. Now it was time for him to remember (literally, "to make to return to the heart"). The reason for hope would be presented in verses 22-24.

Verses 22-24: ⌊Because of⌋ the Lord's faithful love
   we do not perish,
   for His mercies never end.
²³They are new every morning;
   great is Your faithfulness!

**²⁴I say: The LORD is my portion,
therefore I will hope in Him.**

These verses all begin with *cheth*, the eighth letter of the Hebrew alphabet. Verse 22 stands as a good example of Hebrew poetic parallelism, for the second part of the verse repeats in different words the same thought as the first part. The poet recalled God's **faithful love**, which could also be called His **mercies** ("compassions," NIV), a term that suggests emotions stirred up so that action is undertaken for the object of affection. Similarly, **do not perish** can also be expressed as **never end.** Human mercy always has limits, but because God is infinite He extends infinite care—even toward those whose circumstances or sins have put them in a miserable condition.

In verse 23, the term **they** refers to **faithful love** and **mercies.** Like the daily supply of fresh manna every morning that the ancient Israelites enjoyed (see Ex. 16), so the Lord has a fresh supply of love that His people can rely on. Even when people have been faithless and disobedient, the Lord's **faithfulness** is **great.** This text, of course, is the biblical basis for the beloved hymn, "Great Is Thy Faithfulness" (No. 54, *The Baptist Hymnal*, 1991).

Jeremiah had lost his home and possessions. He had nothing except the Lord. Yet with the Lord, he had everything. Thus he declared, **The LORD is my portion.** Because of Jeremiah's confidence in the unfailing love of God, he was certain that his ultimate future lay secure in the Lord's hands. His ringing assurance stands as a challenge for people today to turn to the one true God for **hope.** Those who place their hope **in Him** can be confident that He will welcome them into His eternal presence. The reverse of this is implicit as well: those who have not placed their hope in God can have no expectation that He will be their inheritance when life in this world has ended.

What lasting truths are in these verses?
1. It is not wrong to express your feelings of discouragement to God.
2. Dejected persons should remember what they know is true of God.
3. God's love and faithfulness are infinite and unending.
4. The Lord welcomes those whose hope is anchored in Him.

God Loves When Others Don't (Luke 19:1-7)

What were the social and moral implications of being a chief tax collector? What did Zacchaeus hope to gain by seeing Jesus? What did

Jesus accomplish by reaching out to Zacchaeus? Why did others complain about Jesus' treatment of Zacchaeus? How can this passage help someone to be encouraged by God's love?

The rest of this study focuses on Jesus' well-known encounter with Zacchaeus *[za-KEE-uhs]*, which is found only in Luke's Gospel. Jesus had been teaching and healing for about three years by this time. In fact, He was on His way to Jerusalem where He would accomplish the purpose for which God had sent Him into the world—to die to save sinners. Although the word *love* does not appear in these verses, it is the foundation without which the story does not make sense. God's love through Jesus reached out to an undeserving sinner.

Verses 1-4: He entered Jericho and was passing through. ²There was a man named Zacchaeus who was a chief tax collector, and he was rich. ³He was trying to see who Jesus was, but he was not able because of the crowd, since he was a short man. ⁴So running ahead, he climbed up a sycamore tree to see Jesus, since He was about to pass that way.

Jesus had crossed the Jordan River a few miles from the prominent and ancient Jewish town of **Jericho** *[JER-ih-koh]*. He **was passing through** there to continue on His westward journey to Jerusalem. Great crowds—mainly people from Galilee on their way to Jerusalem to celebrate the Passover—were traveling with the Lord. Nobody, least of all the chief tax collector of the city, expected the love of God to be so wonderfully expressed on that spring day.

It is generally recognized that the Roman system of taxation enabled tax collectors to overcharge the people. The system encouraged cheating. Besides that, Jews who cooperated with the despised Romans were considered traitors against their own people. Jesus was known, however, for reaching out to such people. He welcomed these kinds of people, for many of them recognized that they were spiritually needy. In fact Jesus had included a tax collector, Matthew, among His twelve closest followers (Matt. 9:9; 10:3).

Nowhere else in the Gospels is there a reference to a **chief tax collector.** Zacchaeus evidently supervised a number of other tax collectors who had to give him a percentage of their tax revenues. Thus, it was no surprise that **he was rich.** Nobody knows why **he was trying to see who Jesus was.** Perhaps he had heard about Jesus enjoying a meal in another tax collector's home—something none of the other religious leaders would have dreamed of doing (Matt. 9:10).

My guess is that Zacchaeus had learned about Jesus from one of his tax collector associates. Maybe he had heard about Jesus' stories concerning lost things that were found, sinners who were saved. In Luke 15 Jesus told the parables of the lost sheep, the lost coin, and the lost son, and Zacchaeus may have heard Him at that time.

Curiosity led Zacchaeus to act. **The crowd** surrounded Jesus, but Zacchaeus was **a short man.** He knew that if he didn't act quickly he would miss an opportunity to get a glimpse of this Teacher who did not consider tax collectors to be good-for-nothings. It wasn't hard to guess the **way** that Jesus was **about to pass.** Zacchaeus improvised quickly. He did something that was probably considered undignified for a wealthy adult, but this is an indication of how much he wanted **to see Jesus.** He came to **a sycamore tree.** Native to Israel, these trees grew 30 to 40 feet tall, but they had a short trunk with thick, spreading branches easily capable of supporting an adult. When Zacchaeus **climbed up,** he probably thought he would remain hidden among the leaves. He was in for an abrupt but wonderful interruption of life as he had known it.

Verse 5: **When Jesus came to the place, He looked up and said to him, "Zacchaeus, hurry and come down, because today I must stay at your house."**

This verse demonstrates Jesus' initiative in reaching out in love to an unlovable man. Jesus didn't have to stop, but He did. It startled everyone that **He looked up and said** something remarkable. He called Zacchaeus by name. That by itself would have been enough to demonstrate that Jesus was no ordinary human being. I can imagine Zacchaeus thinking, *How could He know my name?* Before the question could be formed, however, there was more. Jesus asked Zacchaeus to **hurry and come down.** There was no time to waste. Jesus was inviting himself to Zacchaeus's **house.** The phrase **I must stay** reflects a construction in the original that means a divine necessity. It had to happen this way because it was the will of God. Jesus' preaching (see Luke 4:43) and His death (see 9:22) include other examples of this same expression. God was about to bring salvation to someone who did not deserve it, because God's love is the redemptive kind of love.

Verses 6-7: **So he quickly came down and welcomed Him joyfully. ⁷All who saw it began to complain, "He's gone to lodge with a sinful man!"**

These verses contrast two sets of actions and feelings about Jesus. On the one hand is Zacchaeus's joyful response, and on the other hand is the criticism of those in the crowd.

The one who only a few minutes earlier had been, as far as can be known, simply a curiosity seeker, now found himself **quickly** obeying what Jesus had asked him to do. Zacchaeus **came down** from the sycamore tree. He **welcomed Him joyfully** into his house. Over and over in the accounts of Jesus' ministry in the four Gospels is the note of joy. Wherever Jesus reached out and changed lives, it was inevitable that joy followed. In fact, it is not too much to say that whenever people receive the love of God through the gospel, there is joy. Where there is no joy, there has been no reception of the gospel of salvation, which includes the forgiveness of sins and the privilege of personally knowing the Savior.

The widespread hostility of the Jewish people against tax collectors is evident in the way they **began to complain.** The Jews of that day generally recognized that all humans in a certain sense are **sinful.** But tax collectors, prostitutes, and others whose lives did not reflect the basic moral laws of society were publicly called sinners. Typically, the attitude was that God did not and would not love such sinners. Therefore, such people were to be shunned. That Jesus had **gone to lodge** in Zacchaeus's house was scandalous beyond belief, at least in the crowd's opinion. After all, wouldn't it make Jesus ritually unclean to eat with such a sinner?

What the people didn't realize—and what we sometimes forget even today—was that just the reverse had happened. Instead of Zacchaeus making Jesus unclean, Jesus made Zacchaeus clean. Another amazing example of this reversal of expectations had occurred earlier when Jesus healed a man with leprosy by touching him. Instead of the touch defiling Jesus, He made the diseased man whole (Luke 5:12-13; see Lev. 13:45-46).

What lasting truths are in these verses?

1. The love of God in Christ often reaches sinners who are not expecting salvation.

2. It is a divine necessity—the will of God—for Christ to reach out to those who don't deserve it.

3. Those who have never experienced God's love will often criticize expressions of God's mercy.

4. Receiving the love of God includes both obedience and joy.

God's Love Changes Lives (Luke 19:8-10)

How should those who have received God's love in Christ express that they have changed? Why was the use of money an issue? How did Jesus express the purpose of His coming into the world?

Verse 8: But Zacchaeus stood there and said to the Lord, "Look, I'll give half of my possessions to the poor, Lord! And if I have extorted anything from anyone, I'll pay back four times as much!"

Where was Zacchaeus when he **stood there** and spoke to Jesus? Luke did not make this explicit, but this scene probably occurred in Zacchaeus's house after dinner. Luke passed over all the dinner conversation so that he could emphasize Zacchaeus's public statement about his newly changed life. The term **look,** traditionally translated "behold," means that he was drawing attention to the importance of his promise. That he called Jesus **Lord** is evidence that he had now acknowledged Jesus as his new Master.

How would Zacchaeus serve Christ? He would **give half** of his **possessions to the poor.** This was evidence that money no longer had a grip on his life. Jesus had earlier taught, "You can't be slaves to both God and money" (Luke 16:13). A rich man had recently shown himself to be enslaved to money (18:18-23). Zacchaeus was proof that God can break the power of greed.

Zacchaeus had been cured not only of greed but also of swindling. He admitted his guilt in the way he framed the construction **if I have extorted** ("if I have cheated," NIV). His words could well be translated "because I have cheated" or "whomever I have cheated." The principle of justice requires restitution for this crime. The law of Moses required repayment plus a 20 percent surcharge (Lev. 5:16; Num. 5:7). Animal thieves were required to pay back double, threefold, or fourfold (Ex. 22:1-4). Both Roman law and the Dead Sea Scrolls describe cases of fourfold restitution. Zacchaeus accepted the most rigorous understanding of the principle of restitution and personally applied it.

Zacchaeus became a living example of what Jesus had taught in Luke 12:33: "Sell your possessions and give to the poor. Make moneybags for yourselves that won't grow old, an inexhaustible treasure in heaven." The story of Zacchaeus indicates that when people embrace the love of God, expressing that love is the most natural thing in the world. Because Zacchaeus was following the Lord, he now had a different lifestyle.

Verse 9: "Today salvation has come to this house," Jesus told him, "because he too is a son of Abraham."

Jesus in turn made a public response to Zacchaeus's proclamation of a changed life. Although Jesus spoke to Zacchaeus, His point was also intended for the crowd which had grumbled about His associating with a sinner. Jesus had used the word **today** with Zacchaeus earlier (v. 5) when He had invited Himself to Zacchaeus's house. Now He used the same word to affirm His ultimate purpose. It wasn't because Jesus was hungry and wanted a meal. It wasn't because Zacchaeus had something Jesus needed or wanted. It was because Jesus desired to give **salvation.** Of course, He was using the term in its spiritual sense—salvation from sin and death. Salvation is also described as inheriting eternal life and as entering the kingdom of God (Luke 18:18,25-26).

Although Luke didn't tell who the members of Zacchaeus's **house** were, a wife, children, and servants would have been the norm for a rich man. The gift of salvation was for all of them as well. Zacchaeus had expressed the same kind of faith as Abraham, who had believed God and God had counted it to him for righteousness (see Gen. 15:6). Therefore, since Zacchaeus had emulated the faith of Abraham, Jesus called him **a son of Abraham** (see also Rom. 12:9-21).

Verse 10: "For the Son of Man has come to seek and to save the lost."

With this statement, the Lord Jesus summarized His purpose for coming into our world. Some Bible interpreters consider this the key verse for the entire Gospel of Luke. Note that Jesus here called Himself **the Son of Man.** This title for the Messiah (Dan. 7:13) was Jesus' favorite way to refer to Himself. The Jewish expectation about their promised Messiah did not include a Messiah who would **seek** and **save,** but that was why Jesus came.

The verb **seek** implies intentional effort on the part of the one seeking. Jesus had demonstrated such seeking by reaching out to Zacchaeus while he was in the sycamore tree. The purpose of seeking is that people be saved. Those who understand that they are **lost** are truly ready to be found by the Savior. Those who admit that they are sinners are ready to be saved. Those who are discouraged are the most ready to receive encouragement. Jesus' final recorded words to Zacchaeus were similar to what He had said earlier at a great banquet in the house of another tax collector: "The healthy don't need a doctor, but the sick do. I have not come to call the righteous, but sinners to repentance" (Luke 5:31-32).

What lasting truths are in these verses?

1. Those who have truly encountered Christ's love will show it in their lifestyles.

2. Cheating and swindling are sins that will be replaced by generosity and restitution among those who have been saved.

3. All who express faith as Abraham did can be called children of Abraham.

❖ *Spiritual Transformations*

The *Life Question* this lesson seeks to address is, Why should I believe God loves me? The answer has come from studying two very different passages of Scripture. After the author of Lamentations freely expressed his despair, he returned to hope. He expressed confidence that God's faithful love never ends.

Luke recorded Jesus' memorable encounter with Zacchaeus. Jesus reached out with the love of God to one whom society had rejected. Zacchaeus demonstrated his salvation by radically changing his lifestyle from one of greed and cheating to that of generosity and restitution. Zacchaeus stands as a tremendous example that nobody has become so evil that he or she is beyond the possibility of salvation. Jesus is the perfect demonstration of God's love that seeks and saves lost people.

How would you rate your confident assurance of God's love for you?
_____

Whom do you know that needs to know the reality of God's enduring love and with whom you could share the insights from this study?
_____

Are you fully persuaded or is there a Christian friend (or pastor) with whom you would be willing to share your need to be encouraged in this area? _____
_____

Prayer of Commitment: *Dear God, Thank You for the love that You have expressed throughout the centuries to undeserving sinners such as I. Help me to be confident that Your mercies are new every morning. Thank You for loving me even when others don't. Help me show by the way I live that Your love has changed my life. Amen.*

Week of July 11

ENCOURAGED BY SURE SALVATION

EVANGELISM LESSON

Background Passages: 1 John 3:19-24; 5:1-21
Focal Passages: 1 John 3:23-24; 5:1-5,9-13,18-19
Key Verse: 1 John 5:12

❖ *Significance of the Lesson*

• The *Theme* of this lesson is that believers can be encouraged in knowing that their salvation is sure and settled with God.
• The *Life Question* this lesson seeks to address is, How can I know I have salvation?
• The *Biblical Truth* is that evidence of salvation includes obedience to God, love for God and His people, belief in the Son of God, and a life changed by God.
• The *Life Impact* is to help you live with the assurance of salvation.

Can Anyone Really Be Certain of Salvation?

Many in today's society do not acknowledge God's existence. Others, however, accept that there is a God, but they question whether a personal relationship with God is either possible or desirable. They wonder whether such a relationship can be sure and settled. Many people who are faithful in church attendance, even active members of a local congregation, struggle with the issue of whether they are truly saved.

The Bible answers these concerns. Not only does God exist, but He has also done everything necessary for all people to have a saving relationship with Him. Furthermore, the Bible teaches that one can have confident assurance of that salvation.

Word Study: *Born of God* (1 John 5:1,4,18)

"Born of God" combines two terms. First, the Greek verb means "give birth to" ("beget," KJV). The tense of the verb indicates a past action with abiding results. Second is the noun "God." In 1 John 5, the source of birth is God, for the little preposition translated "of" carries the sense of "out of" or "from." Thus, an expanded rendering of "born of God" is "having been born by God's power." This is the new birth, and everyone who is born again has God alone to thank for his or her spiritual life. Through the new birth, sinful human beings can become God's children. Being born of God in reference to believers is found only in John's writings (seven times: John 1:13; 1 John 3:9, twice; 4:7; 5:1,4,18).

❖ Search the Scriptures

The apostle John wrote to a body of believers whom he knew well, probably living in or near the great city of Ephesus. His letter was composed in the A.D. 80s or 90s, and was among the last New Testament books to be written. John had been following his beloved Lord for more than 50 years, and now the aged apostle had learned that false teachings about Christ had infiltrated this church. Some who had been part of the congregation had left the church to follow the false teachers. They were recruiting people from the church, which resulted in doubts and confusion among those in the church. The passages for this Bible study show how John combated false teachings and offered assurance to believers.

Obedience to God (1 John 3:23-24)

What is the relationship between faith and obedience? Between faith and love? How does the Holy Spirit ensure that Christians know that they have a genuine relationship with God?

Verses 23-24: Now this is His command: that we believe in the name of His Son Jesus Christ, and love one another as He commanded us. ²⁴The one who keeps His commands remains in Him, and He in him. And the way we know that He remains in us is from the Spirit He has given us.

The Old Testament contains many specific commands from God. Jesus often clashed with the Pharisees because they mistakenly thought that God's commandments focused on outer conformity rather than on an inner heart that delighted in God (Matt. 23:5). Jesus summarized all these commands as love for God and for others (22:37-40). He also taught, "This is the work of God: that you believe in the One He has sent" (John 6:29). The apostle John may very well have been recalling this in 1 John 3:23-24. Fulfilling God's **command** is a matter of the heart, not simply following a list of do's and don'ts.

Both parts of verse 23 show that salvation is a free gift, not something that can be earned. The first command is to **believe in the name of His Son.** Believing in **Jesus Christ** is the opposite of doing a good work that contributes to salvation. Saving faith—asking Christ to do what we are incapable of doing for ourselves—is the means that God has provided for sinners to be saved.

One of the evidences of trusting in Christ for salvation is to **love one another.** Jesus Himself had **commanded** this in John 13:34: "I give you a new commandment: that you love one another. Just as I have loved you, you should also love one another." Those whose hearts are set ablaze with trust in the loving Savior will automatically overflow in love for others who trust and love Him. The only way to become children of the Heavenly Father is through faith; therefore, it follows that all the children in this great family will love their sisters and brothers, even as they love their Father.

It also follows that **the one who keeps His commands** (to trust Christ and to love each other) is showing that he **remains in Him,** that is, has an ongoing relationship with Christ. This continuing bond is mutual. Christ remains **in him** as well, for Christ is faithful and loving. This is simply His character displayed on behalf of believers.

Thus, part of the evidence of a Christian's salvation is open to observation: Other believers can testify that we love them. Part of the evidence is subjective, experienced in the heart of the believer. The Holy **Spirit He has given us** bears testimony within our very souls that we are children of God. The Apostle Paul put the same truth this way: "The Spirit Himself testifies together with our spirit that we are God's children" (Rom. 8:16). Although believers do not necessarily discern the inner sense of the Spirit at every moment, they should expect from time to time that they would be aware of His presence. God has promised this. The experience of millions of Christians has confirmed it to be true.

An analogy from marriage can clarify this. A husband may not necessarily have the inner sensation of love for his partner at every moment. He should, however, experience such feelings on a regular basis. This is the normal pattern for marriage, and it is terribly sad if a husband loses all feelings for the wife he at one time committed himself to love the rest of his life.

What lasting truths are in these verses?

1. A lifestyle of trusting Christ and loving one another is evidence of salvation.

2. Christ's faithful love causes Him to remain in the lives of those who are saved.

3. The Holy Spirit's inner witness is another evidence of salvation.

Love for God and His People (1 John 5:1-5)

Why is keeping God's commands evidence of salvation? What is the relationship between love for God and love for God's children? How can God's commands not be a burden? What did John mean about faith conquering the world?

Verses 1-2: Everyone who believes that Jesus is the Messiah has been born of God, and everyone who loves the parent also loves his child. ²This is how we know that we love God's children when we love God and obey His commands.

Belief can be understood in a variety of ways. It can refer merely to our assent that something is true. In this way, I believe that there is a devil—and the demons believe that there is a God (see Jas. 2:19). This is not saving faith. In 1 John 5:1 faith means complete reliance on someone. The Christian gospel invites people to depend solely on Jesus the Messiah. Jesus is the One the Scriptures said would come. As the unique Son of God, He opened the way for others to be **born of God** and to become part of the divine family.

In ancient times families were patriarchal, that is, the father was the head and leader—a view not so popular today. Anyone outside the family who loved **the parent** naturally also loved **his child.** (The original reads, "The one who loves the begetter loves the begotten.") How could someone truly love "Mr. and Mrs. Jones" without loving their children? They are all part of the same unit. In the same way, how could someone **love God** and at the same time not **love God's children**? Since **His commands** include the directive that **we love God's children** (see 3:23), we must show that we **love God** by doing just as He has asked.

Verses 3-5: For this is what love for God is: to keep His commands. Now His commands are not a burden, ⁴because whatever has been born of God conquers the world. This is the victory that has conquered the world: our faith. ⁵And who is the one who

conquers the world but the one who believes that Jesus is the Son of God?

Many Christians have struggled with the equation John expressed. How does **love for God** equal keeping or obeying **His commands**? The answer comes by seeing that a heart full of love for the Father delights in pleasing Him. Obedience springs from a heart made alive to God by faith. This kind of obedience is not about seeking to keep an impersonal external standard. Jesus said, "My yoke is easy and My burden is light" (Matt. 11:30). Because of the new birth, the indwelling Spirit enables believers to keep His commands.

The world refers to people antagonistic to God's family (the church), not the world of humanity for whom God sent Jesus (see John 3:16). **The world** seeks to conquer Christians in many ways. Discouragement, defeat, and death are a few. John wrote that **our faith** in Christ could not ultimately be shaken. It is not that **our faith** is strong by itself but that faith unites us to a strong, loving, unfailing God. God's devotion to everyone who **has been born of God** ensures that he or she ultimately **conquers the world.**

In verse 1 John said that a person must believe that **Jesus is the Messiah,** God's Anointed, whom the Old Testament prophets said would come. In verse 5 John referred to **the one who believes that Jesus is the Son of God.** It pleases God for people not only to believe that Jesus fulfilled Scripture, but that He is also the beloved Son of the Father. Such persons have become part of the divine family, and their Heavenly Father will see to it that they are never ultimately defeated by the world.

What lasting truths are in these verses?

1. Saving faith relies wholly on Jesus as the Messiah and Son of God.

2. One aspect of loving God as Father is to love all His children.

3. Far from being somehow sub-Christian, joyfully obeying God's commands is evidence of being born again.

4. God enables all those with genuine faith ultimately to conquer the trials that the world sends.

Belief in the Son of God (1 John 5:9-13)

How important is it to act based on someone's testimony? What kind of testimony is sufficient for someone to trust in Jesus? What is the relationship between trusting in Jesus and eternal life?

Verses 9-11: **If we accept the testimony of men, God's testimony is greater, because it is God's testimony that He has given about His Son. ¹⁰(The one who believes in the Son of God has the testimony in himself. The one who does not believe God has made Him a liar, because he has not believed in the testimony that God has given about His Son.) ¹¹And this is the testimony: God has given us eternal life, and this life is in His Son.**

Not everything in life can be proven with mathematical certainty through scientific experiment or by application of the laws of logic. In general, people are satisfied to act on what they consider to be reliable testimony. Legally, for example, the testimony of two or three witnesses was sufficient to convict someone of a crime in Old Testament times (Deut. 19:15). In everyday life throughout history, people **accept the testimony of men** about what is true. It would be impossible to function without this. Because this is so, people should be much more willing to accept the **greater** witness that God **has given about His Son.** If merely human testimony is good enough for us to act, then **God's testimony** should be all the more persuasive. What has God testified? This is specified in verse 11. The implication, of course, is that we would be foolish indeed not to receive God's testimony as absolute truth.

Verse 10 is a kind of side comment in which John noted the effect of **God's testimony** in two kinds of people. First is **the one who believes in the Son of God.** Such an individual has internal evidence of the truth specified in verse 11. A believer **has the testimony in himself,** because the indwelling Holy Spirit bears witness. The divine testimony is confirmed within the heart of those who have been born of God. Second is **the one who does not believe.** This kind of person denies that **the testimony that God has given about His Son** is true. In other words, unbelievers make **Him a liar.** By their unbelief they are saying that God lied and that He does not give eternal life through Christ. Although John did not develop the idea here, it is surely a very dangerous business to call God a liar.

In verse 11 John clearly stated **the testimony** God has given, which believers know internally but which has now been declared publicly and objectively. First, **God has given us eternal life.** Possibly some of the false teachers upsetting the church were saying that the Christians did not have eternal life. They may have been teaching that the whole concept of eternal life was a myth, something that did not exist. Or they may have been saying that eternal life became a reality in some way without God or Christ having anything to do with it. God has said otherwise, and God's testimony is true.

Second, eternal life is found only **in His Son,** the Lord Jesus. Again, it is likely that John was combating a heresy saying that eternal life can somehow be attained without a relationship with God through Christ. Throughout the ages religious teachers and philosophers have speculated about heaven and the afterlife. God has said that there is no such thing as eternal life apart from a relationship with Christ. People may talk about heaven, but if Christ is not both the *means* of getting there as well as the *goal* of being there, then it cannot be eternal life as God has revealed it.

Verses 12-13: **The one who has the Son has life. The one who doesn't have the Son of God does not have life. [13]I have written these things to you who believe in the name of the Son of God, so that you may know that you have eternal life.**

These two wonderful verses stand together both to *affirm* the truth of the gospel and to *assure* believers that they can know they have salvation. First, John affirmed the relationship between the Son of God and eternal life. He used a pair of logical opposites so that no one could miss the point. First is the positive statement: to have **the Son** is to have **life.** Second is the negative counterpart: to not have **the Son of God** is to not **have eternal life.** Other world religions claim to provide salvation through certain rituals or good deeds or following specified rules. In these religions, salvation is only potential. Adherents never can know for sure whether they have done enough. Only in Christianity is salvation by grace through faith through a personal relationship with Christ. Only in Christ is salvation sure.

Verse 13 is one of the great Bible verses on assurance of salvation. John believed it was possible to **know that you have eternal life.** This study has revealed several ways a person can have assurance of salvation. First is love for one another (3:23). Second is the inner witness of the Holy Spirit (v. 24). Third is love for God (5:2). Fourth is joyful obedience to His commands (v. 2). Fifth is conquering the onslaughts of the world (v. 5). All these, however, are built on the foundation of faith in Christ. All **who believe in the name of the Son of God** are entitled to **know** that they have already received the gift of **eternal life.** Thus, faith—absolute reliance on Christ for salvation—is the divinely appointed means by which we are saved. And those who have been saved will overflow with these evidences of salvation.

John was writing to an audience of confused and troubled believers, not to unbelievers. He was offering them comfort and encouragement by reassuring them of the reality of their relationship with God. His reassurance came in the form of evidences of salvation, which he surely knew to be true among those to whom he wrote. It cannot be stressed too much that all these evidences are never the cause or means of salvation. Salvation is the work of God. As such, no amount of effort on our part can cause salvation—or give assurance of salvation. God has acted to save and to keep the saved secure because that is His character as a loving God.

What lasting truths are in these verses?

1. God Himself has testified that believers in His Son have eternal life.

2. Everyone in a faith relationship with Christ has eternal life.

3. Everyone without a faith relationship with Christ does not have eternal life.

4. Faith in Christ leads to certain evidences of salvation, which in turn give believers assurance.

Life Changed by God (1 John 5:18-19)

Should believers expect that they will reach a point in which they no longer sin? What is the relationship between sin and a believer? Why does a believer need to be kept by God? In what ways do the world and the devil conspire against believers?

Verse 18: We know that everyone who has been born of God does not sin, but the One who is born of God keeps him, and the evil one does not touch him.

In these verses John gave another testimony, another evidence of how God's children may have assurance of their salvation. They have the marks of a changed life. John's wording in verse 18 has been the subject of great debate. Some, unfortunately, have asserted that John affirmed that saved persons—**everyone who has been born of God**— could reach a point where they no longer sin. Is it possible to attain complete moral and spiritual perfection in this life? This interpretation runs counter to the teachings of Scripture elsewhere, that believers never reach such a point in this life. Just two verses earlier (v. 16), John referred to a brother who commits a "sin that doesn't bring death." Earlier in his letter, John affirmed that believers must continue to deal with sin in their lives (see 1 John 1:8,10).

The correct interpretation of verse 18 can be understood by noting the nature of the present tense verb translated **does not sin.** In Greek, the present tense carries the sense of an enduring or ongoing action. Thus, **does not sin** means "does not continue to sin (as a lifestyle)." Here's how one commentator expressed it: "If John means that Christians do not sin in any way, then he contradicts what he said previously in these verses. Rather John is indicating that Christians do not sin in such a way as to be characterized by such behavior. They sin, but they are not in bondage to sin as to be controlled by its power."[1]

The last part of verse 18 does not mean that a believer will not experience satanic attacks. Paul had instructed the Ephesian Christians to "put on the full armor of God so that you can stand against the tactics of the Devil" (Eph. 6:11). The verb **touch** here implies striking someone with the result of harming or destroying. The emphasis is on Christ, **the One who is born of God,** who is mighty enough to keep from harm His brothers and sisters who have also **been born of God.** Those who have taken shelter in Christ can have absolute confidence that those whom He has saved He also keeps—forever.

Verse 19: **We know that we are of God, and the whole world is under the sway of the evil one.**

This verse, like the preceding one, begins with **we know,** a verb that emphasizes certainty based on trustworthy evidence (testimony). Not only do believers have changed lifestyles that are no longer characterized by sin, but they also have God as the source of their lives. The phrase **of God** is the same one used in every instance of the phrase **born of God** in this study. Christians have changed families. **The evil one,** the Devil, has his family, and **the whole world is under** his **sway.** The people of the world have a lifestyle of sin, which is characteristic of the Devil's family members. That way leads to death. The people born of God have a lifestyle of not sinning, which is characteristic of God and His whole family. Because Christ the Son of God lived a sinless life and died so that sinners could live, those who have become the sons and daughters of God—born of God through the new birth—have had their lifestyles changed by God. They are no longer characterized by sin but are seeking to become more like Christ. Such people have assurance that they have received eternal life.

What lasting truths are in these verses?

1. Christ has promised to keep from satanic injury all who have been born again.

2. The lifestyle of those born again will not be that of habitual sinning.

3. There is an observable contrast in the lifestyles of those who are of God and those who are under the sway of the Devil.

❖ *Spiritual Transformations*

The *Life Question* this lesson seeks to address is, How can I know I have salvation? The answer has come from studying parts of 1 John. When the apostle wrote to these believers, he instructed them that the connecting link between believing in Christ and loving one another is simply obeying God's commands. He emphasized that those who have trusted in Jesus—the Messiah and the Son of God—have been born of God. They have become part of God's family and therefore desire to obey their Father because they now love Him. Such people have lifestyles transformed by God, and Christ assures them of their salvation—their eternal life with Him.

What evidences in your own life give you assurance that you have eternal life? _____
_____

Are you certain that you have been born of God? If so, summarize the time and circumstances here. _____
_____
_____

If you are not sure of your salvation, you can place your faith in Christ right now. Read the material inside the front cover of this periodical and follow the guidelines printed there.

Do you know someone who is struggling with salvation, either someone unsaved or someone without the assurance of salvation? In the space that follows, note how you could share the message of this study with that person. _____
_____

Prayer of Commitment: *Lord Jesus, Thank You for the salvation that comes by trusting in You. Thank You for the evidences of salvation that You give to believers and for the assurance of my salvation. Amen.*

[1]Daniel L. Akin, *1 John* in *The New American Commentary*, vol. 38 (Nashville: Broadman & Holman Publishers, 2003), 212 (footnote 252).

ENCOURAGED BY REDEMPTIVE USEFULNESS

Background Passage: Nehemiah 1:1–2:18
Focal Passages: Nehemiah 1:2-7,10-11; 2:4-8,17-18
Key Verse: Nehemiah 1:11

❖ *Significance of the Lesson*

• The *Theme* of this lesson is that we can be encouraged in knowing that God can use us, regardless of our past or present circumstances.

• The *Life Question* this lesson seeks to address is, How can I be useful when I feel so useless?

• The *Biblical Truth* is that the Lord can use anyone who depends on Him, regardless of circumstances, including distance, opposition, or one's position in life.

• The *Life Impact* is to help you live as a useful servant of God.

Useful? Me?

Some of my church friends struggle to believe that God wants to use them. Henry is self-conscious that he never went to college after high school. Judy, a single mom, feels that her failed marriage has disqualified her from service. Greg has a speech impediment. Maria and Ricky face opposition from both sets of parents, who think they should just "get over" the idea of serving the Lord. You too may be thinking, *There's no way God can use me.* Scripture teaches that God uses people who have weaknesses and limitations. Relying on God rather than focusing on circumstances determines a person's usefulness to God.

Word Study: *Favor* (Neh. 1:11)

The Hebrew noun *racham* is similar to the noun *chesed* (see Word Study for the week of July 4). In Lamentations 3:22 the two terms parallel each other. *Racham* occurs less than 50 times in the Old Testament. It is most often used to refer to the compassion that God shows to His people in caring for them and providing forgiveness for their sins (see Ps. 51:1). Occasionally the term is applied to the compassionate treatment people have for others (see Gen. 43:30; Zech. 7:9). *Racham* occurs four times in Nehemiah in the great prayer of confession by the Israelites, remembering God's past mercies (9:19,27,28,31). The only other instance of *racham* in the book is when Nehemiah asked God to make the king willing to extend him favor (1:11).

❖ *Search the Scriptures*

One of the most tragic events of the Old Testament period was the destruction of Jerusalem by the Babylonians in 586 B.C. About 50 years later the Babylonians were defeated by the Persians. The Persians allowed the Jewish exiles to return to their homeland. The Jews built a modest temple for worshiping the Lord and dedicated it about 516 B.C., 70 years after Solomon's glorious temple was ruined. The city of Jerusalem, however, was still in shambles. Debris was everywhere. The city walls—so important for security—had not been repaired. Into this situation came Nehemiah. God used this Jewish employee of a pagan king to accomplish His purposes for the city of Jerusalem, despite overwhelming circumstances.

Assess the Situation (Neh. 1:2-3)

What did Nehemiah learn that was so devastating? Why would it have been disgraceful to live in an unwalled city?

Verse 2: Hanani, one of my brothers, arrived with men from Judah, and I questioned them about Jerusalem and the Jewish remnant that had returned from exile.

One of the Persian capital cities was Susa (1:1), located in what is now southwest Iran. There Nehemiah lived as a Jew who had descended from the original exiles. The king of Persia ruling from Susa at the time was Artaxerxes. His 20th year to rule was about 445 B.C. (see 2:1). This means that the returned Jews had been living in Jerusalem for about 70 years since their temple had been restored.

Nehemiah was at this time an important official in King Artaxerxes's household. He served as the royal cupbearer. According to ancient historians, the cupbearer was responsible to taste the king's wine to be sure it contained no poison. Obviously Nehemiah had proven himself to be trustworthy and reliable, for the king's life depended on him.

Hanani [huh-NAY-nigh] was a fellow Jew, who later became a supervisor over the wall-building project (Neh. 7:2). Whether he was one of Nehemiah's biological **brothers** or simply a fellow Jew is unknown. He **arrived with men from Judah** at the Persian city of Susa one December day. (Kislev corresponds generally to December; see 1:1.) Nehemiah was curious **about Jerusalem.** Now there was no king. Only **the Jewish remnant that had returned from exile** lived there, eking out an existence as a people subject to Persia.

Verse 3: They said to me, "The survivors in the province, who returned from the exile, are in great trouble and disgrace. Jerusalem's wall has been broken down, and its gates have been burned down."

Nehemiah soon learned about both the people and their physical situation. **Jerusalem's wall** had been **broken down, and its gates** had been **burned down** by the Babylonians about 140 years earlier. Of course, Nehemiah knew about that. He likely assumed that the situation had recently been corrected (see Ezra 4:7-23). He soon learned otherwise. People living in an unwalled city were subject to **great trouble** by any threatening enemy. Further, it was a **disgrace** for the people who belonged to an all-powerful God to be living in such sad circumstances.

It is well said that we cannot meet a need (spiritual or otherwise) until we learn about that need. Nehemiah was surely not expecting to be confronted with a need that day. New information, however, is often how God stirs up His people to accomplish His purposes.

What lasting truths are in these verses?

1. Sometimes God brings crucial information to us through ordinary sources such as a brother.

2. When we learn about a spiritual or physical need among others, God may wish to use us to help meet that need.

Confess Sin (Neh. 1:4-7)

Why was Nehemiah's first response to weep and mourn? Why was his next response to confess sins?

Verses 4-6a: When I heard these words, I sat down and wept. For a number of days I mourned, fasting and praying before the God of heaven. ⁵I said,

"O Lᴏʀᴅ God of heaven, the great and aweinspiring God who keeps His gracious covenant with those who love Him and keep His commands, **⁶let Your eyes be open and let Your ears be attentive to hear Your servant's prayer that I now pray to You day and night for Your servants, the Israelites."**

The report was not good, and it had an immediate impact on Nehemiah. He seems to have been a man of great feeling. Perhaps it was patriotism; perhaps it was religion; but it did not stop with mere feelings. Nehemiah's actions are expressed with intensity: **I sat down and wept.** Nehemiah also **mourned, fasting and praying.** Throughout the centuries, many of God's people have become so affected by a need that it has become a prayer burden. They simply had to pursue the matter in earnest, sustained prayer. That was Nehemiah's case. He would carry his burden **before the God of heaven.**

Verse 5 and the first part of verse 6 demonstrate the importance of beginning our prayers by acknowledging God's *greatness* and *goodness*, not by bringing Him our sins or our needs first. Notice the greatness of God in Nehemiah's words. (1) He is **the God of heaven.** Other gods claimed to control weather or fertility or health. The Persians worshiped many gods. The true God is sovereign over all things. (2) He is also **great and aweinspiring.** All that He does can cause people to admire Him for who He is. Expressing a high regard for God's greatness is the proper place to begin praying.

Nehemiah also praised God for His goodness. (1) He is the **Lᴏʀᴅ . . . who keeps His gracious covenant.** Nehemiah used the covenant name (**Lᴏʀᴅ** = Yahweh) by which God had revealed Himself to Israel. In His goodness God had reached out to those who did not deserve it. (2) He has **eyes** that **open** and **ears** that can **be attentive.** God sees His people's needs and hears them when they pray—unlike the false gods of other religions.

The greatness and goodness of God means that He desires for those who have known Him to **love Him and keep His commands.** Yet even when people have failed miserably and offended Him, they can still pray. Nehemiah was so earnest in prayer that he came to God **day and night for . . . the Israelites** who were in such need. It will come as no surprise that Nehemiah—the one who felt the burden so intensely—became the instrument God used to meet that need.

Verses 6b-7: "I confess the sins that we have committed against You. Both I and my father's house have sinned. ⁷We have acted very

corruptly before You and have not kept the commands, decrees, or judgments You commanded Your servant Moses."

To **confess** sin is to acknowledge freely that one's acts and attitudes are wrong. Further, true confession is a turning away from these sins. Nehemiah followed the biblical pattern for confession by understanding that sin is primarily **committed against** the Lord. Although sin affects humans and their relationships with others, it is mainly an offense against a holy God. Nehemiah was aware of sins in his own life as well as in his **father's house,** that is, his family. His prayer reflected both the personal and the corporate elements of confession. Sometimes believers today are to confess privately and personally; sometimes they come together to acknowledge their trespasses. Nehemiah understood that God has not left people to guess what pleases Him. He had revealed His will through **commands, decrees,** and **judgments.** These words are all overlapping terms to express the laws that God had **commanded** through His **servant Moses.** This indicates that Nehemiah had the Scriptures available in his own time. This would have included Genesis through Deuteronomy, perhaps more.

Nehemiah knew that when he sinned, it could also be called acting **very corruptly** before God. Sin had corrupted his relationships with God, with others, and with himself. The normal pattern among those God uses is that He cleanses them of sin before He uses them in His service (see Isa. 6:1-8).

What lasting truths are in these verses?

1. God can give people a burden to pray.

2. Recalling God's greatness and goodness is an excellent way to begin prayer.

3. God's people are to confess their sins to Him.

Petition God (Neh. 1:10-11)

What kind of prayer requests did Nehemiah make? Was it selfish for him to ask God for success?

Verses 10-11: **"They are Your servants and Your people. You redeemed ⌊them⌋ by Your great power and strong hand. ¹¹Please, Lord, let Your ear be attentive to the prayer of Your servant and to that of Your servants who delight to revere Your name. Give Your servant success today, and have compassion on him in the presence of this man."⌊At the time,⌋ I was the king's cupbearer.**

Nehemiah's prayer truly is a model that we can follow today. After praising God and confessing sin, he was ready to bring his requests to the Lord. First he prayed for others, and then he prayed for himself.

His prayer for others was explicit. He was aware that he was interceding on behalf of true believers. They were the people God had **redeemed** by His **great power and strong hand.** They were God's **servants** and God's **people.** When we as Christians pray today on behalf of other Christians, we are praying for brothers and sisters in our own family.

Nehemiah asked that God **be attentive to the prayer of Your servant and . . . Your servants.** A further characteristic of those in this spiritual family is that they **delight to revere Your name.** The verb translated **revere** was traditionally rendered "fear," that is, respect or reverence. Although we do not fear God as if He were a tyrant, we fear Him as our Creator and Redeemer and loving Father. Those who forget that "the fear of the LORD is the beginning of knowledge" (Prov. 1:7) have not truly understood who He is or what He has done for them.

At last Nehemiah brought God his personal petition for himself as the Lord's **servant.** He asked for **success** as he initiated the plan that he had formulated. He would need favor from the king, who was his employer. Certainly it is not selfish or self-centered to pray for the success of our service when it is focused not on us but rather on the needs of others.

What lasting truths are in these verses?

1. True prayer includes petitions on behalf of other believers.

2. Prayer may include requests for God to bless our own service for His sake.

Enlist Support (Neh. 2:4-8)

What was so important about Nehemiah's getting the king's support? What is the evidence that Nehemiah had a plan worked out before he asked for the king's help?

Nehemiah waited four months (see 1:1; 2:1) before he enlisted outside help. No doubt he prayed quite often about the situation. His petition to King Artaxerxes shows that he knew exactly what he needed; nevertheless, he was still depending on God to provide that support.

Verses 4-5: **Then the king asked me, "What is your request?"**

So I prayed to the God of heaven [5]**and answered the king, "If it**

pleases the king, and if your servant has found favor with you, send me to Judah and to the city where my ancestors are buried, so that I may rebuild it."

An understandable fear or nervousness marked the day that Nehemiah approached the king for help. He had not in fact asked the king for anything, yet the king understood that Nehemiah wanted something. Nehemiah plainly stated his request, careful to observe the formalities required when speaking to a king. Fulfilling Nehemiah's request could be something that **pleases the king** as well as something to do as a **favor** to one of the king's loyal servants. The request was, **Send me to Judah and to the city . . . so that I may rebuild it.**

Verses 6-8: **The king, with the queen seated beside him, asked me, "How long will your journey take, and when will you return?" So I gave him a definite time, and it pleased the king to send me. [7]I also said to the king: "If it pleases the king, let me have letters ⌊written⌋ to the governors of the region west of the Euphrates River, so that they will grant me ⌊safe⌋ passage until I reach Judah. [8]And ⌊let me have⌋ a letter ⌊written⌋ to Asaph, keeper of the king's forest, so that he will give me timber to rebuild the gates of the temple's fortress, the city wall, and the home where I will live." The king granted my ⌊requests⌋, for I was graciously strengthened by my God.**

The king wanted more specific information about how long Nehemiah planned to be away. This indicates the value that the king put on Nehemiah's service. Nehemiah's careful preparation paid off. He had a **definite time** in mind, and this **pleased the king.**

Nehemiah was not completely finished, however. He wanted more than the king's blessing. He wanted the king to provide him with safe passage as well as material resources to do the work. He would be passing through **the region west of the Euphrates River** (Mesopotamia), which was under Persian control. Therefore he wanted **letters written to the governors** so he could travel safely to Judah. It is appropriate at times for God's people to appeal to their civil government for protection so that they will be enabled to do God's work.

Further, Nehemiah wanted **timber to rebuild.** In particular the temple **gates** and **the city wall** would need this kind of structural support, and so would **the home** that Nehemiah would have to build for himself.

The final sentence beautifully illustrates how God sovereignly works to accomplish His purposes. The balance is careful. On the one hand, **the king granted** Nehemiah's **requests.** On the other hand, Nehemiah

was graciously strengthened by his **God.** God is constantly at work to achieve His purposes, and He chooses to use human beings to do so. He uses pagan kings as well as pious believers.

What lasting truths are in these verses?

1. Careful preparation before asking others to help is a wise approach.

2. Believers should enlist others to help them accomplish "God-sized" tasks.

3. God can and does use a variety of means so His servants will fulfill His purposes.

4. Believers should look for signs of God's gracious hand in blessing their plans.

Encourage Others (Neh. 2:17-18)

Why did Nehemiah inspect the walls before he reported to the officials? What role did Nehemiah expect the officials of Jerusalem to fulfill?

It took Nehemiah several months, perhaps until August, to travel the hundreds of miles from Susa to Jerusalem. His first order of business was to inspect the ruined walls by night, carefully discovering the extent of the damage (2:11-16). After that, he was ready to report to the city leaders.

Verses 17-18a: **So I said to them, "You see the trouble we are in. Jerusalem lies in ruins and its gates have been burned down. Come, let's rebuild Jerusalem's wall, so that we will no longer be a disgrace." ¹⁸I told them how the gracious hand of my God had been on me, and what the king had said to me.**

The people had apparently given in to inertia, accepting things the way they were. Nehemiah's speech would rouse them to action. He identified with the people: **You see the trouble we are in**—note the **we.** He honestly stated the problem: **Jerusalem . . . ruins . . . gates . . . burned.** He told them of their emotional and spiritual danger, that they were a **disgrace.** He informed them of the way Artaxerxes had helped: **what the king had said.** He gave testimony to God's grace: **how the gracious hand of my God had been on me.**

With all these encouragements, he was offering a clear and definite course of action: **Come, let's rebuild Jerusalem's wall.** Surely these principles stand the test of time. God can use us to encourage others, and one way to do so is to speak directly to them, just as Nehemiah did.

Verse 18b: **They said, "Let's start rebuilding," and they were encouraged to ⌊ do ⌋ this good work.**

Nehemiah had toiled hard to overcome obstacles to usefulness. He had overcome the distance. He had overcome the king's questions. He had overcome his job situation. He had overcome other resistance as well (2:10,19). Nehemiah's speech worked. The people of Jerusalem **were encouraged to do this good work.** Surely Nehemiah's heart sang for joy when he heard them say, **Let's start rebuilding.** They completed the building of the wall in only 52 days (see 6:15).

What lasting truths are in these verses?

1. Encouraging others includes identifying with others and telling them honestly what their needs are.

2. Testimonies of God's grace in our experience will encourage others.

3. People often respond enthusiastically when they are offered a clear and definite course of action.

❖ *Spiritual Transformations*

The *Life Question* this lesson seeks to address is, How can I be useful when I feel so useless? The life of Nehemiah illustrates how this can be accomplished. After he became aware of a need among God's people, he began by taking his burden to the Lord. His earnest prayer is a model of praise, confession of sin, and petition—both for others and for himself. Finally, with a specific plan in mind, he enlisted support (from the king) and encouraged those already in Jerusalem to join him in the work. As it was with Nehemiah, so it is with us. God wants to use us—and He will do so when we rely on Him and make ourselves available for His use.

Which of the lasting truths in this lesson speaks most to you?

_____

Whom do you know that you might encourage with the message of this study? _____

What could you personally do during the next week to help you live as a useful servant of God? _____

Prayer of Commitment: *Dear God, Thank You for the examples of people like Nehemiah. You used him despite the circumstances, and I now affirm that You want to use me despite my circumstances. Today and from now on I make myself available for You to do so. Amen.*

ENCOURAGED BY FAITHFUL HOPE

Background Passage: Habakkuk 1–3
Focal Passages: Habakkuk 1:2-6,12-13; 2:2-4,18-20; 3:17-19a
Key Verses: Habakkuk 2:20

❖ *Significance of the Lesson*

• The *Theme* of this lesson is that we can be encouraged in knowing that God offers us hope in the midst of a violent world.
• The *Life Question* this lesson seeks to address is, Where can I find hope in the midst of violence and injustice?
• The *Biblical Truth* is that the righteous person who lives by faith can have hope in God regardless of the human or natural circumstances around him.
• The *Life Impact* is to help you live with hope in God.

The World Is Such a Hopeless Mess

War in Iraq. Acts of terrorism in many of the world's cities. Child abductions. Corporate greed and scandal. SARS and AIDS. Earthquakes and hurricanes and tornadoes. Where is God?

There is a biblical answer to this question. God acts in and through the details of history—even our own personal histories—to accomplish His purposes. He is not bound to act when and how believers desire. We can, however, confidently have hope in Him, no matter how grim the circumstances surrounding us appear to be.

Word Study: *Violence* (Hab. 1:2-3)

The Hebrew noun *chamas* is found 60 times in the Old Testament. It means "violence," particularly the cruel or unjust kind. The result of such violence was death or destruction. The related verb can be translated "to treat violently" or "to do violence." The element of lawlessness or trampling on others is implied. Habakkuk used *chamas* six times (1:2,3,9; 2:8,17 [twice]) in his book. In these occurrences, the larger context indicates God's solemn pledge to judge those guilty of *chamas.* The term could well be applied to all the cruelties so evident in today's world.

❖ *Search the Scriptures*

Almost nothing is known of the prophet Habakkuk *[huh-BAK-kuk]* except that he wrote a brief but profound Old Testament book. Assyria was in power and had just conquered the Northern Kingdom of Israel (721 B.C.) The Southern Kingdom of Judah had weathered attacks from the Assyrian army. Habakkuk wrote sometime after Babylon (Chaldea) had risen to power (Hab. 1:6) but before Babylon attacked Judah. According to historians, the Babylonians conquered Assyria in 612 B.C. and began attacking Judah within a few years.

Habakkuk is unlike most biblical prophetic books, which usually focus on God's urgent pleas to the Israelite people through the prophet. Instead, Habakkuk recorded a dialog between himself and God in which he asked God questions and God answered him. God's replies are as relevant today as they were 2,600 years ago.

Violence Abounds (Hab. 1:2-4)

What was the nature of Habakkuk's complaint? What does it suggest about the social and moral conditions of his time? Who are **the wicked** *and who are* **the righteous** *in verse 4?*
Verses 2-4: How long, LORD, must I call for help
  and You do not listen,
or cry out to You about violence
  and You do not save?
³Why do You force me to look at injustice?
  Why do You tolerate wrongdoing?
Oppression and violence are right in front of me.
  Strife is ongoing, and conflict escalates.
⁴This is why the law is ineffective
  and justice never emerges.
For the wicked restrict the righteous;
  therefore, justice comes out perverted.

As Habakkuk looked at his homeland, the country of Judah, he saw that the rich and powerful were getting away with corruption. Society around him was marked by **violence** and **injustice** and **oppression** and **wrongdoing** and **strife** and **conflict.** All these terms are different ways of describing the outrageous sins rampant in the land. The term **violence** summarizes them all, and all of them piled together suggest the nightmare of wickedness in Habakkuk's day. It was more than he could bear. Sin was committed brazenly, **right in front of** the prophet. Evil was **ongoing.** In fact, it was getting worse: **conflict escalates.**

On the one hand, the power brokers in society were **wicked.** Instead of encouraging **the righteous** to do what was fair and good, they were making it hard on them. The poor were getting cheated. In the words of the prophet, **justice comes out perverted.**

On the other hand, God seemed to be doing nothing to restrain wickedness. In verse 2 the prophet protested to God that he had long cried out **about violence,** but God had done nothing to save the righteous from the violent. The prophet also voiced his concern that God apparently didn't **listen** to him. Thus, the opening to his prayer is like a sigh or complaint: **How long, LORD, must I call for help?**

Habakkuk was open and honest to pray this way. His words do not express a lack of faith or giving up on God. He understood his relationship to God clearly enough to know that he could express his concern freely without sinning against Him.

What lasting truths are in these verses?

1. There are times when God permits wickedness to go unchecked.

2. Praying with honesty may sometimes include voicing a protest to God about the prominence of injustice and social evil.

God Is at Work (Hab. 1:5-6)

What was God's answer to Habakkuk's complaint? Is it right to see the hand of God in world events? in past events in our personal lives?
***Verses 5-6:* Look at the nations and observe—**
be utterly astounded!
For something is taking place in your days
   that you will not believe
   when you hear about it.
⁶Look! I am raising up the Chaldeans,
   that bitter, impetuous nation
that marches across the earth's open spaces
   to seize territories not its own.

These verses are the Lord's answer to Habakkuk's concern. God will not allow evil and injustice to go on forever. Sooner or later there will be a reckoning, for God in His very nature is just. God had a plan to deal with it—yet one that would cause the prophet to **be utterly astounded.** God would choose to work through **the nations** to accomplish His purposes for Judah. Habakkuk was invited to **observe,** and in all probability the prophet lived to see the fulfillment of God's promise. The prophecy would involve something soon—**in your days**—and unexpected—**that you will not believe.** Ordinarily we expect that restoring justice and peace will be the best way to deal with injustice and violence. This time, however, God would send someone even more unjust and more violent than the evil leaders of Judah. Those who were wicked were about to be overwhelmed by those who were even more wicked.

God was in charge of all the nations, with their military plans and political maneuverings. This means He was responsible for **raising up the Chaldeans** (the Babylonians). Habakkuk had only to watch what the Babylonians were about to do. They were ruthless—a **bitter, impetuous nation.** Further, they had their mind set on expansion—**marches across the earth's open spaces** seizing **territories not its own.** History records that the Babylonians did all this. Three times the Babylonians invaded Judah, culminating in 586 B.C. with the destruction of Jerusalem and the burning and looting of the temple (2 Chron. 36:17-20). The answer that God gave was one the prophet could not have wanted—and against which he would lodge his next complaint.

The same kind of thing happens in our day. We can see an unfair situation—and the thing that replaces it is even more distressing than the original circumstance. This happens in all societies—even the safest. The tragedy of 9/11 has led to an American society in which homeland security is always a major concern. Just as Habakkuk was called on to see God's hand in the coming of the Babylonians, so we too are called on to see that God is at work in the world today.

What lasting truths are in these verses?

1. God is at work in all circumstances.
2. Sometimes God's answer to prayer is difficult to accept.

The Righteous Suffer (Hab. 1:12-13)

What titles for God did Habakkuk use in his prayers? What moral dilemma was Habakkuk expressing in these verses?

Verses 12-13: **Are You not from eternity, Yahweh my God? My Holy One, You will not die. Lᴏʀᴅ, You appointed them to execute judgment; ⌊my⌋ Rock, You destined them to punish us. ¹³⌊Your⌋ eyes are too pure to look on evil, and You cannot tolerate wrongdoing. So why do You tolerate those who are treacherous? Why are You silent while one who is wicked swallows up one who is more righteous than himself?**

Habakkuk faced a number of truths that he was having difficulty reconciling. Again, he openly told God his concerns. Notice the different titles by which he addressed God: **Yahweh** or **Lᴏʀᴅ,** the covenant-keeping God of Israel; **my God,** the One whom the prophet knew personally; **My Holy One,** the God who is always just; **my Rock,** the One on whom Habakkuk could depend. The prophet also knew that God was from eternity and would not die. God is always present to see everything and cannot be defeated.

This great God is also **too pure to look on evil,** a truth that brought forth Habakkuk's next complaint: **So why do You tolerate those who are treacherous? Why are You silent?** Habakkuk's dilemma was the same as ours. Sometimes God's actions seem to be unfair. Sometimes righteous people suffer unjustly. Sometimes the wicked are the ones who appear to be having the last laugh by enjoying their unrighteous behavior to the fullest extent.

What lasting truths are in these verses?

1. Believers should remain confident that God is holy and will not tolerate evil.

2. Sometimes God permits the more evil to punish the less evil.

3. Questioning God about this can be done in a righteous way.

Live by Faith (Hab. 2:2-4,18-20)

What was God's response to Habakkuk's second compliant? What is the relationship between the reality of judgment and living by faith?

Verses 2-4: **The Lᴏʀᴅ answered me: Write down this vision; clearly inscribe it on tablets so one may easily read it.**

³For the vision is yet for the appointed time;
   it testifies about the end and will not lie.
Though it delays, wait for it,
   since it will certainly come and not be late.
⁴Look, his ego is inflated;
   he is without integrity.
   But the righteous one will live by his faith.

Habakkuk's first question had been, "God, why is unrighteousness in Judah flourishing?" God's answer was, "I will punish this evil through the Babylonians." The second question was, "God, how can You use the more evil (Babylon) to punish the less evil (Judah)?" **The LORD answered** the prophet with a new **vision.** (The word for **vision** is used specifically for God's revelation to a prophet.) The truth was not for the prophet alone. He was to **clearly inscribe it on tablets** for publication. Others could **easily read it** as well—both original readers and later people such as ourselves.

The vision was that Babylon too would be judged for its evil, at **the appointed time.** God gave the prophet insight about **the end** of Babylon, and the revelation could **not lie.** There would be **delays,** so Habakkuk and the people of Judah must **wait for it.** At the time God designated, judgment **will certainly come** on Babylon and would **not be late.** Daniel 5 records God's judgment on Babylon, which occurred about 539 B.C., more than 60 years after Habakkuk's prophecy.

Babylon would be destroyed not only for its wicked deeds but also for its evil intentions. Because **his ego is inflated** and **he is without integrity,** he will be judged.

On the other hand **the righteous one** will not be ultimately destroyed but **will live,** even though he must express patient trust. The upright person does not trust in anything of this world. He has confidence in God and expresses this **by his faith** in God. The New Testament quotes the latter part of this verse in support of salvation by faith alone (Rom. 1:17; Gal. 3:11; Heb. 10:38). The principle is clear. The circumstances of life may appear overwhelming. Only by confidently trusting in God is there hope—either for this life or for eternity.

Verses 18-20: **What use is a carved idol**
   after its craftsman carves it?
It is ⌊only⌋ a cast image, a teacher of lies.
For the one who crafts its shape trusts in it
   and makes idols that cannot speak.

¹⁹Woe to him who says to wood: Wake up!
   or to mute stone: Come alive!
Can it teach?
   Look! It may be plated with gold and silver,
   yet there is no breath in it at all.
²⁰But the LORD is in His holy temple;
   let everyone on earth
   be silent in His presence.

In verses 18-19 the prophet sarcastically showed the foolishness of idolatry. How stupid it was for **a carved idol** to be worshiped by the very **craftsmen** who **carves it**! How utterly useless it was for a **cast image** to be trusted in by **the one who crafts its shape**! The one who trusts in **idols that cannot speak** or supposes that **mute stone** has the possibility of coming alive is trusting in the wrong thing. Such a religion is **a teacher of lies.** Habakkuk asked, **Can it teach?** The answer is, Never! Of course, there was a certain hideous beauty attached to many idols. The statues were **plated with gold and silver.** But no one should mistake beauty for truth. No matter how exquisite the workmanship that went into idols and their temples—ancient or modern— **there is no breath in it at all.** The truth is found only in the living God.

The righteous who have faith in God and live a life of faithfulness to God have chosen His way. They have chosen the way of the true and living Lord. He is **the LORD** who is **in His holy temple** (see Ps. 11:4; Rev. 4:1-11). The idols of false religions are silent before those who would worship them. Nevertheless, **everyone on earth** must **be silent in His presence** when He judges. No one can successfully raise an objection to what God accomplishes in the end. People of faith—such as Habakkuk and believers of today—may express their concerns to Him. People without faith may shake their fists in His face. But ultimately God's intention is that "every mouth may be shut and the whole world may become subject to God's judgment" (Rom. 3:19).

What lasting truths are in these verses?

1. Every evil is subject to God's ultimate judgment, even though it may appear to be delayed.

2. God will judge sins of the spirit such as conceit as surely as activities such as violence.

3. The righteous are to live by faith in God.

4. Idolatry is foolish because idols are powerless.

Hope in God (Hab. 3:17-19a)

What was the nature of Habakkuk's final prayer? What was the basis of his hope?

Verses 17-19a: Though the fig tree does not bud
and there is no yield on the vines,
though the olive crop fails
and the fields produce no food,
though there are no sheep in the pen
and no cattle in the stalls,
¹⁸yet I will exult in the LORD;
I will rejoice in the God of my salvation!
¹⁹The LORD my Lord is my strength;
He makes my feet like those of a deer
and enables me to tread on mountain heights!

After the Lord answered the prophet's questions, he was completely satisfied. Habakkuk's response has become a model for God's people throughout the ages: worship through reverent prayer. All of Habakkuk 3 is a wonderful poetic prayer in which ringing confidence in God is expressed. God had warned him that the Babylonians were coming. The circumstances in Judah would become grim. Yet the Lord's holiness would cause Him to bring Babylon to judgment. The prophet confessed his trust in the Lord.

In verse 17 the prophet outlined a number of disasters that might occur to devastate an agricultural society. Famine could cause these things. So could the coming of an invading army, such as the Babylonians. The first four disasters focused on disruption of the cycle of plant life. He mentioned four sources of food staples for the ancient Israelite diet: **fig tree, vines, olive crop,** and **fields.** Without figs for sweetness and grapes for wine and olives for cooking oil and wheat or barley for bread, there would be little way to lead a normal life. Disaster might overtake the herds as well. The prophet envisioned the complete loss of the domestic animals used for food and clothing. **Sheep in the pen** might be lost, and **cattle in the stalls** might die or be stolen.

Because the prophet had experienced the reality of God's answer to him in 2:4, the circumstances were of secondary importance. Habakkuk's strong statement of hope in God, despite evil and suffering, is one of the greatest declarations in Scripture. It is the Old Testament equivalent of Paul's powerful affirmation in Romans 8:28.

Habakkuk closed with five truths. The first two are his response to the Lord's greatness; the third one is about the Lord's power; and the last two are about what the Lord would do for him. **I will exult in the LORD** expresses that he was completely satisfied with God rather than with God's gifts. **I will rejoice in the God of my salvation** shows that he had personally experienced God. Salvation wasn't abstract for Habakkuk. When he received salvation, he received God, and this brought him joy. **The LORD my Lord is my strength** was Habakkuk's confession that God would be strong for those who confess that they are weak and rely solely on Him. **He makes my feet like those of a deer** is a beautiful picture of confidence in God during life's journey, for deer are quite agile creatures. Finally, God **enables me to tread on mountain heights,** which recalls David's certain hope in God when the Lord delivered him (see Ps. 18:33). Although the circumstances were conspiring to take the prophet into the valley of despair, his absolute confidence in God enabled him to ascend the pinnacle of hope.

What lasting truths are in these verses?

1. God's people are not exempt from difficult circumstances.

2. Difficult circumstances are a good time to find joy in God.

3. The God who saves His people also gives them the strength they need.

4. God gives confident hope to those who trust in Him.

❖ Spiritual Transformations

Habakkuk expressed his confident hope in God even though the circumstances were grim (violence, injustice) and might become even worse (destruction of crops and herds). He rejoiced in the God of his salvation who gave him strength.

What could you personally do during the next week to express your hope in God?

_____

_____

Prayer of Commitment: *Dear God, Thank You that You are always working in every circumstance, even when I can't see it, even when violence abounds and the righteous suffer. Help me to live by faith in You. Help me come to hope in You with the same confidence that Habakkuk expressed. Amen.*

Study Theme

Peter's Principles for Successful Living

What is your measure of success? Is it having beautiful children or grandchildren? Is it your career or home? Maybe you measure success by the size of your financial assets. If any of these is your primary measure, you are settling for a cheap substitute for what you could have. Success in the Bible is understood from an entirely different perspective than in society. Why settle for fool's gold when you can have the real thing?

A great way to learn about the biblical outlook on success is through observing the life and teachings of one of the true success stories in Scripture, the Apostle Peter. Nobody looking at this brash young commercial fisherman would have taken a second glance at him. Yet Peter rose from the obscurity of Galilee to become the rock-solid leader of Christ's apostles. Not only did he lead the early church in Jerusalem successfully, but he also went on to travel widely as a preacher, teacher, and missionary. Before he died Peter wrote two inspired letters that Christians have been learning from for almost two thousand years. We have much to learn from Peter!

Whatever successes you have had, this study of Peter's experiences as a disciple and his teachings are sure to challenge you. The studies for this month focus on five important principles from the Apostle Peter. First we will be introduced to Peter in his early days as a disciple, seeing him as one who learned to live in a relationship with the Lord Jesus (Aug 1). Second, we will look at the first few verses of Peter's first letter to learn about living confidently as Christians (Aug. 8). Third, we will consider what Peter taught about achieving success by acting in ways that God desires (Aug. 15). Fourth, we will learn that humility is an asset, not a liability, for those whom God calls successful (Aug. 22). Finally, we will consider how to express faithfulness and courage in our allegiance to Christ (Aug. 29).

KNOW JESUS

Background Passages: Matthew 4:18-20; 14:22-33; John 1:35-42
Focal Passages: Matthew 4:18-20; 14:25-33; John 1:40-42
Key Verses: Matthew 4:19-20

❖ *Significance of the Lesson*

• The *Theme* of this lesson is that successful living begins with a relationship with Jesus Christ.

• The *Life Question* this lesson seeks to address is, What does a personal relationship with Jesus involve?

• The *Biblical Truth* is that a personal relationship with Jesus Christ involves spiritual transformation, discipleship, and faith.

• The *Life Impact* is to help you live in relationship with Jesus Christ.

How Is Success Related to Knowing Jesus?

Have you ever heard the saying, "It's not *what* you know but *who* you know that counts"? Often this has to do with gaining access to someone or something. My teenage son landed his first real job because he knew the company owner, a church friend of ours. Another time our family received great concert tickets because we knew the lead performer. Years ago I was introduced to Billy Graham by a mutual friend.

Success in life can be measured in many ways, but as God defines it, it's not *what* you've done or *how much* you have. It's who you know. True success begins with coming to know Jesus. But knowing Him is much more than just knowing about Him. It involves spiritual transformation, just as Simon Peter, the Galilean fisherman, discovered.

Word Study: *Follow* (Matt. 4:19)

Two Greek words are translated with the one word **follow** in Matthew 4:19 and are more literally "come after." The word for "after" occurs 36 times in the New Testament, either as an adverb or as a preposition. It normally has one of two senses. First, it could mean "after" in regard to time, in the sense of "later." Thus, John the Baptist pointed out Jesus as "the One who is coming after me" (Matt. 3:11). Second, as used in Matthew 4:19, the term could mean "after" in regard to place, in the sense of "behind." Thus, Jesus was asking His disciples literally to walk behind Him as He traveled the roadways of Galilee. They learned by observing Him in the most direct fashion. Later on, the disciples realized that this meant following behind Him not literally but spiritually—trusting Him, learning from His example, and obeying His teachings.

❖ *Search the Scriptures*

The central character of the four Gospels is, of course, the Lord Jesus. The stories of other people mattered only as they related to Him, whether His friends (such as John the Baptist or Mary Magdalene) or His enemies (such as King Herod or the Pharisees). Thus, the story of Peter's growing relationship with Jesus must be pieced together from several episodes in which he played a role. In this study three such incidents will demonstrate this for us. We will begin by studying Peter's first encounter with Jesus, move on to the period when he began to follow Jesus full time, and then consider the occasion in which Peter's faith in Christ was fully displayed. The later lessons in this study theme will focus on Peter's insights after a lifetime of following Jesus.

Be Changed by Jesus (John 1:40-42)

At what point was Jesus in His ministry when He first encountered Peter? How did Peter learn about Jesus? What was the implication of the name change from "Simon" to "Cephas"?

Verses 40-42a: Andrew, Simon Peter's brother, was one of the two who heard John and followed Him. ⁴¹He first found his own brother Simon and told him, "We have found the Messiah!" (which means "Anointed One"), ⁴²and he brought Simon to Jesus.

John's Gospel did not report either the baptism or the temptation of the Lord Jesus. John began telling about Jesus' ministry after He had returned from the wilderness temptation to the area "across the Jordan, where John was baptizing" (John 1:28). Right away John the Baptist began pointing people to Jesus as the Lamb of God. One of the first was a Galilean fisherman named **Andrew,** who **heard John and followed** Jesus. Andrew spent enough time with Jesus that same day to become convinced that Jesus was the long-promised Messiah (vv. 37-40).

Andrew had a **brother** named **Simon,** the short form of Simeon, a common Hebrew name. (See 2 Pet. 1:1, in which he used the longer form to introduce his letter.) The good news he discovered in Jesus was too much for Andrew to keep to himself. Apparently he knew just where Simon was, so he went to Simon and said, **We have found the Messiah!** This implies that Andrew and Simon had been looking forward to the long-promised Messiah. Andrew knew after he had met Jesus that their search was over.

The Gospel writer explained to those readers unfamiliar with Hebrew or Aramaic that **Messiah,** a Hebrew term, **means "Anointed One."** In Greek, the language in which the Gospel was composed, the equivalent word was "Christ." Thus, the Hebrew noun **Messiah** is *Christos* in Greek and comes into English as **Anointed One.** The coming Messiah was predicted in many Old Testament passages. A couple of places where the actual Hebrew term for "Messiah" or "Anointed One" is used are Psalm 2:2 and Daniel 9:26.

Andrew **brought Simon to Jesus** in the literal sense. This would prove to be only the beginning of a lifetime that Simon Peter walked with Jesus spiritually.

Verse 42b: When Jesus saw him, He said, "You are Simon, son of John. You will be called Cephas" (which means "Rock").

Upon meeting Simon, Jesus gave him an unexpected pronounce-ment. He called him by his birth name **Simon** and identified him in the ordinary Jewish manner of noting also his father's name **John** (which was an alternate form for Jonah; see Matt. 16:17). This is simply to say that Jesus knew exactly who and what Simon was. Yet Jesus also realized what Simon would become after he had fully come to know Him. He no longer saw an ordinary fisherman; He saw the **Rock.** The Aramaic term for **Rock** is **Cephas**; the Greek term is *petros* (Peter).

We should remember that **Cephas** was a nickname, and wherever the New Testament uses the name we should mentally note it as "Rocky" or a similar English nickname. People normally receive a nick-name after the characteristic of the name has been observed—for example, "Blondie" or "Red." Peter received his nickname beforehand. As the rest of the Gospels show, Peter's natural temperament was hardly rock-like. He was reckless and unpredictable. He grew into the nickname that Christ had given him at the beginning. Only after Christ's resurrection did Peter become the steady, solid leader of the early church that was implicit in Jesus' nickname for him. Only Christ could bring about such a change.

What lasting truths are in these verses?

1. Jesus is the Messiah promised in the Old Testament.

2. We should stay alert to introduce family members and friends to Jesus.

3. Jesus can change one's natural temperament into something much stronger.

4. Jesus knows what we are and what we will become.

Follow Jesus (Matt. 4:18-20)

Why had Peter returned to his fishing business? What was the nature of Jesus' call to Peter and Andrew? What did it mean to be **fishers of men**?

Verse 18: As He was walking along the Sea of Galilee, He saw two brothers, Simon, who was called Peter, and his brother Andrew. They were casting a net into the sea, since they were fishermen.

After his first encounter with Jesus, Peter returned to his family's fishing business on **the Sea of Galilee.** Scripture is silent about when and why this happened. As a married man, perhaps Peter was simply feeling his natural responsibility to provide for his family's needs (see Matt. 8:14-15.) When Jesus relocated His ministry to Galilee (John 4:1-3), He encountered **Simon . . . and his brother Andrew** for a second time. Surely the brothers didn't expect anything more than another opportunity to visit with Jesus when they saw Him **walking along the Sea of Galilee.** They were fishing according to the method preferred by commercial **fishermen** of that day, by **casting a net into the sea.** It was a demanding but honest way to make a living.

Verses 19-20: "Follow Me," He told them, "and I will make you fishers of men!" ²⁰Immediately they left their nets and followed Him.

Jesus' command, **Follow Me,** could be translated literally "Come after Me." This clarified for Simon Peter and Andrew that having a personal relationship with Jesus involved more than just knowing about Him. It meant more than even following His teachings. It included responding to His call to follow Him as a continual part of their lives.

Jesus promised that following after Him meant they could expect to have an eternal impact for good in the lives of others. He used language relevant to their occupation. Instead of just catching fish, they would become **fishers of men.** Peter became the instrument through whom thousands of people came to faith in Jesus Christ. This began only a few months later, when Jesus sent out Peter and the other apostles two by two (Mark 6:7). Acts 2 records another dramatic example of how this happened on the day of Pentecost. The two letters from Peter written to early Christians show that he was still fishing for men over 30 years later.

Peter and Andrew responded to Jesus' challenge instantly. Verse 20 simply records that they obeyed—completely and at once. **They left their nets,** the representative of their old lives. They came after Him, literally at first, following the roadways as He led the way—even to the point of His arrest. Later on, they would learn how to follow Him after He returned bodily to heaven, the way that people today follow Him. Just as Jesus only hinted at what following Him would mean for Peter, so today He does not tell people in advance everything that the exciting adventure of following Him will mean. Yet just as surely as Peter's life would never be the same after he obeyed the call to follow Jesus, so it is today. The call to come after Him is not limited to so-called "full-time Christian workers." All believers are expected to follow Jesus in this way.

1. An initial encounter with Jesus is only the start of a lifetime of following Him.

2. Jesus wants everyone to follow Him.

2. Those who follow Jesus should look forward to being involved in introducing others to Him.

Trust Jesus (Matt. 14:25-33)

What did Peter's walk on the water reveal about his faith? How did this incident strengthen Peter's understanding of the identity of Jesus? How should the relationship between trusting Jesus and worshiping Him be understood?

Verses 25-26: **Around three in the morning, He came toward them walking on the sea. ²⁶When the disciples saw Him walking on the sea, they were terrified. "It's a ghost!" they said, and cried out in fear.**

By this time Peter had been a full-time follower of Jesus for a number of months. Jesus had designated him as one of the twelve apostles (Matt. 10:1-4). Jesus' reputation as a great teacher and a worker of miracles had resulted in great throngs of people crowding around Him. The climax to this was Jesus' feeding of the five thousand using only five loaves and two fish (Matt. 14:13-21). That evening Jesus asked His apostles to get on board a boat and launch out on the Sea of Galilee. During the night, a furious storm suddenly engulfed the lake with wind and waves that tested the skill and nerves of even professional fishermen. Panic overtook them.

It was about **three in the morning,** six hours or more since the disciples had last seen Jesus. Our imaginations may fill in a few of the blanks. The disciples were likely worn out from rowing against the wind and too tired to think clearly. Perhaps a sudden break in the clouds allowed a bit of moonlight to fall on Jesus as **He came toward them walking on the sea.** We should not suppose that the disciples believed in ghosts any more than modern believers do, although there were Jewish superstitions about ghosts in the night. But the strain was just too much. What else were they to think of the moonlit figure **walking on the sea**?

Matthew portrayed their reactions vividly. Since the apostle Matthew was there, he recalled something that was no doubt still vivid in his mind as he wrote his Gospel years later. First, emotionally wrung out, **they were terrified.** Second, they gave voice to their fears: **It's a ghost!** Further, they **cried out in fear.** Perhaps the lesson for us is that even when Jesus' followers do exactly what He asks them to do, there may come frightening—even life-threatening—experiences. Jesus never promised that following Him would remove people from difficulties. Sometimes Christ's followers experience more trouble after they begin following Him than before.

Verse 27: **Immediately Jesus spoke to them. "Have courage! It is I. Don't be afraid."**

Jesus **immediately** sought to soothe them. He addressed the three fears the disciples had expressed. The words **Have courage!** spoke to their emotional frenzy. The term can be translated "cheer up" or "take heart." In John 16:33 Jesus used the identical word when He said, "Take courage! I have conquered the world." On that occasion they could more readily believe His word because they had already seen Him conquer the stormy sea.

The phrase **It is I** is literally "I am," the phrase with which Jesus identified Himself on other occasions (John 8:58: 13:19; 18:5). This was no ghost but Jesus Himself, the "I AM." It is probable that the disciples understood Jesus' use of this phrase as a claim to be God, because "I AM" was the name of God that He had revealed to Moses (Ex. 3:14). Note also that the disciples would worship Him as the divine Son of God when He got into the boat (Matt. 14:33). Jesus' words **Don't be afraid** spoke directly to their fears. Matthew showed how Jesus' words in verse 27 precisely countered the concerns of verse 26.

Verse 28: **"Lord, if it's You," Peter answered Him, "command me to come to You on the water."**

Although two other Gospel writers told about Jesus' walking on the water (Mark 6:45-52; John 6:16-21), only Matthew described Peter's bold action. Since it really was Jesus (not a ghost) and since Jesus was showing that He was the master over the ordinary laws of nature (by walking over the waves), then why shouldn't Jesus **command** that Peter walk out to Him **on the water**?

I have often wondered whether Peter instantly thought he was a fool. If I had been one of the other disciples present in the boat, I would have thought, *He's gone completely crazy!* Jesus, however, would reward Peter's faith. It wasn't that Peter had great faith but that he had a great Lord.

Verses 29-30: **"Come!" He said.**

And climbing out of the boat, Peter started walking on the water and came toward Jesus. [30]But when he saw the strength of the wind, he was afraid. And beginning to sink he cried out, "Lord, save me!"

Jesus' command to **come** was all Peter needed. Peter began to do what no other mere mortal has ever done: he **started walking on the water and came toward Jesus.** During the past two centuries or so, it has been fashionable for many "enlightened" people to ridicule this event as impossible. But Matthew meant to present this as a miracle from God. Jesus is Lord over nature's laws, and He can bend them to do His will. If He chose for Peter to walk on water in a faith response to the command to **come,** then His power would see to it that Peter would indeed walk on water. Whatever Jesus commands, He enables. I wish I had been there to see Peter **climbing out of the boat.** Perhaps the other disciples began to think that Peter wasn't such a foolhardy soul after all. Where was their faith?

Many sermons have been preached on verse 30. Peter could only see **the strength of the wind** by taking his attention off Jesus. Jesus had told him to come and he came. Yet the negative circumstances made him **afraid** once more. His faith faltered and Peter began **to sink.** His attention instantly returned to Jesus. Just as surely as Peter had **cried out** when he thought he saw a ghost, now he **cried out** (same verb) when he thought he was going to drown. No matter how challenging the circumstances, it's never wrong to cry out to Jesus. No more heartfelt prayer was ever offered than, **Lord, save me!** He had just acknowledged Jesus as his Lord from inside the boat (v. 28); now he called on Jesus as Lord from outside the boat.

Verses 31-32: **Immediately Jesus reached out His hand, caught hold of him, and said to him, "You of little faith, why did you doubt?"** [32]**When they got into the boat, the wind ceased.**

Jesus' tone of rebuke must have been gentle when he called Peter **you of little faith.** In the original language it is a single word, "little-faith-one," which Jesus used several other times to challenge His followers to trust Him more completely (Matt. 6:30; 8:26; 14:31; 16:8; Luke 12:28; see also Matt. 17:20). The question **why did you doubt?** was one for which Jesus already knew the answer. The idea behind the question was so Peter would reflect on the lesson Jesus was teaching him. Peter realized that Jesus knew about his doubts. Peter had not trusted Jesus completely. Whenever our faith in His Word falters, we may be sure that Jesus will prompt us with the same question. Such prompting is meant to increase faith, not to belittle it. "Little-faith" always has the potential of becoming "great-faith," but "no-faith" will never succeed. Jesus' plan is that the faith of His people will grow.

That day had been filled with miracles—from the feeding of the multitude to the two men walking on the water. There was one more to come. Peter and Jesus climbed **into the boat** amid the raging waves. Then suddenly, **the wind ceased.** Not only was Jesus powerful enough to walk over the waves, but He was also powerful enough to stop them whenever He wanted to. This was actually the second time that the disciples had witnessed Jesus' power over a storm on the Sea of Galilee (8:23-27).

Verse 33: **Then those in the boat worshiped Him and said, "Truly You are the Son of God!"**

Here is not only the climax to the account of Jesus' walking on the water, but it is also the fitting culmination to this study of Peter as he grew in a personal relationship with Jesus.

At the beginning, Peter literally went to Jesus in response to Andrew's belief that Jesus was the long awaited Messiah. Later, Peter had become so persuaded of Jesus' importance that he began following Him full time. After that, Peter was designated by Jesus as one of the inner group of twelve apostles. In the present account, Peter had marvelously shown his trust in Jesus and had called Him "Lord" two times (vv. 28,30). Jesus was Peter's "Lord" in the sense of "Master" or "Mentor" or "Teacher."

Thus far Peter and the others—so far as is recorded—had not reached the conclusion that Jesus was worthy to be **worshiped.** After this, however, there could be no doubt in their minds that the One who called Himself "I Am" was **truly . . . the Son of God.** This is the first time in Matthew's Gospel account that the disciples had made such an affirmation. They were beginning to understand what they had learned about Jesus. In the Old Testament, it was not perfectly clear that the promised Messiah would also be the Son of God. But now Peter and **those in the boat** reached the right conclusion. Later Peter would make this connection explicit in his famous confession, "You are the Messiah, the Son of the living God" (16:16).

The only suitable response for human beings who have become aware of the presence of God is to bow in reverent worship. Peter and all **those in the boat worshiped Him.** The tumult of the storm—in the sea and in their hearts—had been replaced by the tranquility in which genuine worship could occur. The verb translated **worshiped** is literally "bow down," and in the New Testament it is most often used in the sense of reverent worship of God or Christ.

Thus far in Matthew's Gospel, the wise men, a man with leprosy, and a leader named Jairus had bowed before Jesus (Matt. 2:11; 8:2; 9:18; see Luke 8:41). Now, for the first time (but not the last), His disciples bowed in worship before Him, not only as Messiah and Lord, but also as the Son of God.

What lasting truths are in these verses?

1. Whenever life situations become hard, Jesus can overcome those difficulties.

2. By believing Christ's word and acting on it, believers can do what is humanly impossible.

3. Focusing on problems rather than on Christ can lead believers into grave danger.

4. Jesus is the "I Am," the Son of God who deserves to be worshiped.

❖ Spiritual Transformations

The *Life Question* this lesson seeks to address is, What does a personal relationship with Jesus involve? The answer has come from studying three episodes in the life of Simon Peter during the time of Jesus' public ministry.

In Simon's first encounter with Jesus, He gave him the new name Peter. This signaled that knowing Jesus always includes being changed or transformed into something more wonderful than we were before. Of course, these transformations occur over long periods of time. On a later occasion, Jesus asked Peter to follow Him. This indicates that knowing Jesus is more than knowing about Him. It is intentionally letting Him be the Master or Leader of our lives. Even later, Peter demonstrated his faith in Jesus' word by getting out of the boat and walking on the water. This shows that knowing Jesus means growing in faith. It means moving from being "little-faith" to "greater-faith."

Which of the lasting truths in this lesson speaks most to you?

_____

_____

What did you learn about the Apostle Peter that you did not know before? _____

_____

Describe the evidence in your own life that you know Jesus.

_____

_____

This study has shown three important aspects of living successfully. Evaluate your own success in these three areas by rating yourself from 1 (unsuccessful) to 5 (very successful).

1 2 3 4 5 I have been changed by Jesus.

1 2 3 4 5 I intentionally follow Jesus day by day.

1 2 3 4 5 I am growing in my faith in Jesus.

What actions should you take during the coming week to become more successful in these areas? _____

_____

Prayer of Commitment: *Lord Jesus, Thank You for the example of the Apostle Peter. Help me know You as he knew You. I commit myself to following You and trusting in You. Amen.*

LIVE CONFIDENTLY

Bible Passage: 1 Peter 1:1-12
Key Verses: 1 Peter 1:8-9

❖ *Significance of the Lesson*

• The *Theme* of this lesson is that successful living includes living confidently in the resources God provides.
• The *Life Question* this lesson seeks to address is, What factors enable me to live with more confidence as a Christian?
• The *Biblical Truth* is that God makes His resources available to believers so that they can live confidently even in the midst of trials.
• The *Life Impact* is to help you live confidently as a Christian.

How Is Success Related to Confident Living?

What does it mean to have confidence? I checked the dictionary built into my computer, and the terms "self-assurance" and "self-reliance" popped onto the screen. All of us have met persons who simply ooze with confidence that they can deal with any problem using their own resources. But we also know individuals so affected by world events or by crises in their own lives that they have retreated into despair and hopelessness. Christians are not immune to having doubts and apprehensions when faced with events that seem beyond their control.

True Christian confidence is possible and desirable. It is the assurance that God—not self—provides the resources needed to deal with every challenge. Believers who learn such confidence will inevitably experience God's definition of successful living.

Word Study: *Distressed* (1 Pet. 1:6)

The Greek verb *lupeo* originally meant "to have pain" from such things as hunger, cold, disease, or injury. Its meaning was easily transferred to refer to pain in one's heart or soul caused by what others say or do (sad news, insults, getting sick, death); thus, it came to mean "to feel sorrow, grief, or distress." The apostles were grieved when Jesus said that one of them would betray Him (Mark 14:19). *Lupeo* occurs less than 40 times in the New Testament. Its most concentrated appearance is in 2 Corinthians 2:2-5; 7:8-9, in which Paul spoke of the distressing relationship between the Corinthian Christians and himself. In John 16:20 Jesus provided the key to understanding the grief that the difficulties of life send. The only time Peter used *lupeo* in his letters was 1 Peter 1:6, with exactly the same sense as in John 16:20. Christians can endure pain since they know that sorrow and distress are inevitable but they are also temporary.

❖ *Search the Scriptures*

By the time Peter wrote his first epistle more than 30 years had passed since Jesus' crucifixion, resurrection, and ascension. While Jesus was on earth bodily, Peter had been able to follow Him constantly. Peter continued to follow Jesus after His ascension. The good news of Christ had spread out from Jerusalem to the far corners of the Roman Empire in an amazingly short time. House churches had sprung up in most major cities.

At the same time, many believers faced persecution because of their faith in Christ. Peter had learned about a number of disciples in the province of Asia (modern-day Turkey) who needed hope and encouragement. His inspired letter has been enabling Christians ever since to live confidently even in the midst of trials.

The Divine Initiative (1 Pet. 1:1-2)

To whom was Peter writing? What did he mean by the phrase **temporary residents***? How did he relate the Father, the Son, and the Holy Spirit to salvation?*

Verses 1-2: Peter, an apostle of Jesus Christ:

To the temporary residents of the Dispersion in the provinces of Pontus, Galatia, Cappadocia, Asia, and Bithynia, chosen [2]according to the foreknowledge of God the Father and set apart by the Spirit for obedience and for the sprinkling with the blood of Jesus Christ.

May grace and peace be multiplied to you.

Peter identified himself as **an apostle of Jesus Christ** (see Luke 6:12-14). Jesus had chosen Peter to be one of His representatives, so

Peter exercised his authority in many ways. One way was to write letters to believers. He followed the normal letter-writing pattern of his day. Letters began by noting first the author and then the recipients, followed by a greeting. Only then did the substance of a letter appear.

Peter called the first readers **temporary residents of the Dispersion.** The language he used had been applied originally to Jews scattered from their homeland after the Babylonian captivity (Esth. 9:30). Here, however, Peter was thinking of the Christians—both Jews and Gentiles—spread out all over the world, whose temporary home was earth but who were waiting for their heavenly home (1 Pet. 5:10).

The term **chosen** shows God's initiative in all matters of salvation. The confidence of Christians is based not on believers but on God's plan and His execution of the plan. Peter included each of the Persons of the Trinity in our salvation (see Eph. 1:3-14). **God the Father** is the One who planned salvation before the beginning. His **foreknowledge** included not only that Christ would save but also the believers themselves. God will not be surprised by anyone who is in heaven. He has **chosen** them. **Jesus Christ** is the One who shed His **blood,** securing the salvation of sinners. After people are saved, **obedience** to Him becomes a characteristic of their lives. **The Spirit** is the One who applies the work of Christ in an individual's life. Believers have been **set apart** by the Spirit so they can grow in holiness and the ability to obey Christ more fully.

Peter's greeting implied much more than a friendly hello. He mentioned both **grace** (God's initiative in reaching out to undeserving sinners) and **peace** (the wholeness resulting from salvation). These are available without limit to believers, for it is **multiplied** to them by God's inexhaustible supply.

What lasting truths are in these verses?

1. Every Christian is a temporary resident of earth, waiting for heaven.

2. God has initiated everything for our salvation.

3. The Holy Spirit has set believers apart for holy living.

4. God's grace and peace are available in limitless supply.

The Living Hope (1 Pet 1:3-5)

*What gifts connected with salvation did Peter emphasize for believers? What is the connection between new birth and inheritance? What did he mean by a **living hope**? In what ways are believers not yet saved?*

Verses 3-5: **Blessed be the God and Father of our Lord Jesus Christ. According to His great mercy, He has given us a new birth into a living hope through the resurrection of Jesus Christ from the dead,** [4]**and into an inheritance that is imperishable, uncorrupted, and unfading, kept in heaven for you,** [5]**who are being protected by God's power through faith for a salvation that is ready to be revealed in the last time.**

Because of what he had already stated in verses 1-2, Peter had much for which he **blessed** (or praised) **God.** He continued to note a number of added blessings, some that believers have already received, but others for which believers wait. All these are the result of God's **great mercy,** which is another way of speaking of His grace. Not only does God desire to express mercy, but He also has the infinite **power** to do so (unlike other people or gods). Only a high price, the death and **resurrection of Jesus Christ from the dead,** made God's mercy fully operational.

What gifts has God already bestowed on believers? One is the **new birth.** Jesus' famous nighttime discussion with Nicodemus is the most famous biblical passage about the new birth (John 3:1-21), also called "regeneration." Jesus referred to it as being "born again" (v. 3) and "born of the Spirit" (vv. 6,8). No one has ever been responsible for his natural birth, for he owes it to his parents. So it is with spiritual birth. The Heavenly **Father of our Lord Jesus Christ . . . has given us** this birth. Peter was still emphasizing God's initiative in everything concerning salvation.

Another gift is **a living hope.** The opposite of this is a dead or worthless hope, such as other religions and philosophies offer. The term **hope** in the New Testament means a firm assurance about some future event. This is unlike English usage, in which hope usually means wishful thinking. Peter used "hope" five times in his letter (1:3,13,21; 3:5,15). When believers truly experience the gospel, they receive hope for a secure future as a present possession. Such hope is safe because **the resurrection of Jesus** is an absolute certainty. Peter expressed the content of the believer's hope in verse 4.

A third gift is being **protected by God's power.** God did not save sinners and abandon them, any more than a good mother would give birth to a child and then abandon it. The God who regenerates has more than enough mighty power to give believers confidence and assurance. Interestingly, however, Peter balanced **God's power** with the believer's

faith. Just as God does not save sinners without belief in Christ, neither does He protect them contrary to their faith. The two walk hand in hand. Thus we can see that God has already provided all that believers need in order to live confidently as Christians throughout this life.

But there is much more. God has promised us certain gifts for the future, and Peter mentioned two of them here. The first future gift is **an inheritance.** In the normal passage of time, children born into a family sometimes receive an inheritance when their parents die. Any number of circumstances (financial disaster, parents changing their wills) may keep such an inheritance from becoming a reality. The believer's eternal inheritance, however, is already in existence. It has been guaranteed already by **the resurrection of Jesus,** and it awaits the believer's resurrection.

Peter described with three words the nature of this inheritance in contrast to earthly ones. (1) The heavenly future is **imperishable**; stated positively, it is perpetual. (2) The heavenly future is **uncorrupted**; stated positively, it is pure. (3) The heavenly future is **unfading**; stated positively, it is permanent. This perpetual, pure, permanent gift already exists. It is simply **kept in heaven** for believers. Although Scripture offers only glimpses of what life with Christ will be like after we die, they are enough to make us long for it. What a wonderful contrast to every earthly inheritance!

The second future gift is that our **salvation** is **ready to be revealed.** There is more than just heaven to enjoy when we die. At Christ's return, **in the last time,** believers will participate in the resurrection, receiving fully glorified bodies just like His. This is what Peter meant by "the grace to be brought to you at the revelation of Jesus Christ" (1 Pet. 1:13). Although we ordinarily think of salvation as that which happened when we first trusted in Christ, there is also a future aspect to it. Paul wrote, "Our salvation is nearer than when we first believed" (Rom. 13:11; see also Rom. 8:23). This salvation occurs at the return of Christ, at which time we will enjoy the eternal blessings that come to those who are citizens of His kingdom by faith.

What lasting truths are in these verses?

1. The present blessings of salvation include new birth, living hope, and protection by God's power.

2. The future blessings of salvation include a perfect inheritance in heaven and the resurrection body at Christ's return.

3. Believers are to praise God for such wonderful blessings.

The Inexpressible Joy (1 Pet. 1:6-9)

What is the relationship between trials and the genuineness of our faith? What should be the relationship between faith and sight as it relates to salvation? How can joy be inexpressible?

Verses 6-7: You rejoice in this, though now for a short time you have had to be distressed by various trials ⁷so that the genuineness of your faith—more valuable than gold, which perishes though refined by fire—may result in praise, glory, and honor at the revelation of Jesus Christ.

Because of God's gifts to believers, they **rejoice.** In God's good plan for them, however, **various trials** come to believers. The original readers had been **distressed** by their circumstances, which included persecution. As 21st century readers, our griefs may come from many sources. Both our bodies and our spirits are exposed to pain, but God has a wonderful purpose. He intends that every trial should be a means for proving **the genuineness of** believers' **faith.** One of the great Old Testament examples of a person's faith being tested was when God asked Abraham to sacrifice his son Isaac (Gen. 22). God is free to use both the normal hassles of life as well as direct persecution as means of such testing. We would never know how strong our faith has grown if it were never tested.

Peter used a well-known example from the testing of precious metals. **Gold** is **refined by fire** in order to prove that it is really gold, not imitation gold. Gold is thought of as permanent, but it too will pass away at the end of the world. If people go to the trouble of testing metal **which perishes,** then one can understand why God puts the believer's faith, which is **more valuable than gold,** to the test.

God is surely aware that sometimes the test feels like **fire.** He does not test believers as an end in itself; rather, He knows that such tested faith will **result in praise, glory, and honor** to the Lord Jesus at His **revelation** (second coming). In any event, such tests are only **for a short time.** What should believers make of events that seem out of control? They are actually part of God's magnificent plan that will enable them to honor Jesus more fully; therefore, they can **rejoice.**

Verses 8-9: You love Him, though you have not seen Him. And though not seeing Him now, you believe in Him and rejoice with inexpressible and glorious joy, ⁹because you are receiving the goal of your faith, the salvation of your souls.

Peter had seen Jesus with his own eyes. Neither his readers nor we have **seen Him.** This is no barrier to a relationship with Christ. Peter may have been thinking of Jesus' last beatitude: "Blessed are those who believe without seeing" (John 20:29). Christians **love Him;** they **believe in Him and rejoice.** The verb **love** *(agapao)* is the great biblical word for love in its highest form; the word **believe** *(pisteuo)* is the verb form of the noun translated **faith** in verse 9.

Christians who know Christ can have **inexpressible and glorious joy.** This joy is the opposite of the distress or sorrow caused by various trials. God intends trials to result in joy rather than grief. This seems like a paradox; perhaps for that reason it is **inexpressible**—nobody can fully explain it—but it is nonetheless real. Further, it is **glorious,** because it looks forward to the time that **the goal of . . . faith** will be fully realized: **the salvation of your souls.** Here, **souls** stands for the whole person, because Peter was certainly not excluding the resurrection of the body from the experience of salvation. The living hope is sure; therefore, the joy is already expressed. Christians have the right to be the most joyful people in the world!

What lasting truths are in these verses?

1. Various trials are normal experiences for believers in this life.
2. God intends that trials will reveal the genuineness of our faith.
3. Tested faith brings honor to the Lord Jesus.
4. Even under trials, believers can be filled with a joy that is hard to explain.

The Revealed Gospel (1 Pet. 1:10-12)

How much did the Old Testament prophets understand about the gospel? Why are Christian believers in a better position than the prophets of old were?

Verses 10-11: Concerning this salvation, the prophets who prophesied about the grace that would come to you searched and carefully investigated. ¹¹They inquired into what time or what circumstances the Spirit of Christ within them was indicating when He testified in advance to the messianic sufferings and the glories that would follow.

Believers in Christ have received a richer, fuller experience of **salvation** than the Old Testament saints received. For one thing, we live in a time after the price of salvation has been paid by Christ. This was a matter that **the prophets who prophesied** understood to a certain extent. They knew that **grace would come** in a more complete form than they had experienced it. They knew that salvation was to be based on **the messianic sufferings** (see Ps. 22 and Isa. 53). They also recognized that there would be **glories that would follow** the sufferings of Christ. Peter did not specify these **glories,** but he knew the ancient prophecies of Christ's resurrection (Ps. 16:8-11; see Peter's citation in Acts 2:25-28) and ascent to heaven (Ps. 110:1; see Peter's citation in Acts 2:34-35).

Peter was also affirming that Christ has already modeled the very pattern that his readers were going through: suffering as the pathway to glory. Thus, believers of all centuries have been encouraged by observing that the One who saved them has Himself been "distressed by various trials" (1 Pet. 1:6)—and has come through them to rejoicing and glory.

How could **the prophets** know these things? **The Spirit of Christ within them was indicating** the truth to them. To put it in modern terms, Peter was connecting the Old Testament with the New Testament. The same Holy Spirit of Christ who inspired the biblical prophets now works in believers. The focal character for both Testaments is **Christ.** There has always been one divine plan of salvation, and that is through Christ Jesus. The gospel fully revealed in the New Testament was no novelty; rather, it is something in harmony with Old Testament revelation.

Peter was aware, however, that the Old Testament prophets did not know everything about the coming of Jesus. They did not know **what time** the Messiah would be born—therefore most Jews were unaware of His birth when it finally happened. They also did not know **what circumstances** would surround the Messiah's coming—such as His birth in a stable and His childhood in the small town of Nazareth (Luke 2:7; John 1:46). The prophets **inquired** about this, but it was hidden from them. Similarly, the same thing is true for us concerning Christ's second coming. The fact of His return is clear; the time and circumstances are mainly hidden, no matter how much we inquire.

Verse 12: **It was revealed to them that they were not serving themselves but you concerning things that have now been announced to you through those who preached the gospel to you by the Holy Spirit sent from heaven. Angels desire to look into these things.**

The prophets also recognized that their ministries were not limited to their own times. The Spirit who inspired them to preach and write **revealed to them that they were not serving themselves,** that is, the people of their own time. They were also serving those who would live after the fulfillment of their prophecies.

The fulfillment of the biblical prophets' promises has **been announced** through **those who preached the gospel.** Peter was himself one of these preachers. On the day of Pentecost **the Holy Spirit** was **sent from heaven,** not only to empower Christian preaching but to enable Christian living (Acts 2). The same Spirit of Christ who inspired the biblical prophets has now become the permanent, indwelling gift to all who have believed in Christ (Rom. 8:9). Thus, the Holy Spirit's ministry has helped Christian believers to have a clearer understanding of God's plan of redemption than the prophets of old had. He has done this in several ways:

- The Spirit inspired the prophets with true (but incomplete) details about salvation.
- The Spirit empowers preachers to announce the gospel in this present age.
- The Spirit enables believers to respond to the message and effects the new birth.
- The Spirit indwells believers to live confidently, even in the midst of trials.

With his mysterious comment about the angels, Peter highlighted the importance of the gospel as now revealed to believers. Because the holy angels of God have not sinned, they do not need a Savior as fallen humans do. Jesus taught, however, that they rejoice over sinners who repent (Luke 15:10). They are intrigued by salvation and eagerly **look into** how God's plan of salvation is being accomplished.

Angels were visibly present on the day of Jesus' birth and resurrection (Luke 2:9-14; 24:4-8). They appeared at strategic times in the early church (Acts 5:19; 8:26; 12:7). Their interest is apparently not limited to the earliest days, because the verb **desire** is in the present tense. Peter was reminding his readers—and therefore us—that there is an unseen heavenly host tracking our progress as we grow in the experience of believing, loving, obeying, and rejoicing in the Lord Jesus. God will not let His holy angels be disappointed. He will see to it that His people will "result in praise, glory, and honor at the revelation of Jesus Christ" (1 Pet. 1:7).

What lasting truths are in these verses?

1. The Old Testament prophets understood the gospel to include the sufferings of the Messiah and His later glory.

2. Since Christ has already come, Christian preachers proclaim a fuller understanding of the gospel than the Old Testament prophets did.

3. The Old Testament prophets had the same Spirit working in them as do Christian preachers today.

4. The gospel of Christ, which is of interest to the angels, changes the lives of those who receive it.

❖ Spiritual Transformations

The *Life Question* this lesson seeks to address is, What factors enable me to live with more confidence as a Christian? This study, from the opening verses of the First Epistle of Peter, has highlighted several factors. Together they show that God has provided all the resources needed for successful living. First, God Himself has initiated our salvation. Christ's sacrificial death and the Spirit's work of setting believers apart owe everything to God. Second, God has given such gifts as new birth and living hope in the present so that believers will be assured of their future blessings. Third, trials are God's means of proving the integrity of believers' faith—which brings joy that cannot be expressed in words. Finally, Peter has shown that the gospel message, now fully revealed, gives a clearer understanding of God's plan of salvation than the prophets ever had.

How would you now answer the Life Question for this study?

_____

How would you describe the living hope in your own life?

_____

Whom do you know that you might encourage to live confidently as a Christian? How will you do that? _____

_____

What will you do during the coming week to help you express your own confidence in the resources God has provided?

_____

Prayer of Commitment: *Dear God, Thank You for giving me everything I need to live confidently as a Christian. Help me to measure this confidence not by my own self-reliance but by trusting Your resources. Amen.*

ACT RIGHT

Background Passage: 1 Peter 1:13–2:12
Focal Passages: 1 Peter 1:13-16,22-25; 2:1-3,11-12
Key Verse: 1 Peter 1:15

❖ *Significance of the Lesson*

• The *Theme* of this lesson is that successful living includes living in holiness.

• The *Life Question* this lesson seeks to address is, How should I act as a Christian?

• The *Biblical Truth* is that the Christian life is to be marked by holiness, love, maturity, and honor.

• The *Life Impact* is to help you act in the ways God desires.

How Is Success Related to Acting Right?

"Pastor, I'm always yelling at the kids, and it's not their fault. I know I'm saved, but I just can't do anything about my temper."

"Pastor, I'm sure I'm going to heaven, but I'm hooked on cable TV. Lately I've been watching a lot of 'adult' entertainment late at night. That doesn't matter, does it?"

Pastors and church leaders have heard many confessions similar to these. Some churchgoers think that salvation is only about going to heaven when they die. Others have confessed Christ as Savior, but they live ungodly lives—no different from their unsaved neighbors. They need to learn what Peter taught about the kind of actions God desires from them. God's definition of success includes living in holiness *now*. Although the world will disagree, God calls successful those who live in holiness.

Word Study: *Holy* (1 Pet. 1:15,16)

The Greek adjective *hagios* is related to the verb *hagiazo*, which means "to set apart." This word family occurs about 280 times in the New Testament and always refers to things or persons set apart by and for God. God Himself is holy because nothing and no one is like Him. Many things and persons that God has set apart for His special purposes are called holy in the New Testament: "holy city" (Matt. 4:5); "holy mountain" (2 Pet. 1:18); "Holy Scriptures" (Rom. 1:2); "holy angels" (Mark 8:38); "holy apostles" (Eph. 3:5). Also, the Holy Spirit is referred to 90 times in the New Testament. It is striking that in the New Testament believers in general are called "holy ones," traditionally translated "saints." All believers in Christ have a special relationship to God, who has set them apart for Himself.

In 1 Peter, *hagios* occurs eight times. Three times the reference is to the holiness of God (1:12,15,16). Twice the term occurs in an exhortation concerning the behavior of believers (1:15,16). Twice the term describes believers ("holy priesthood," 2:5; and "holy nation," 2:9). The final reference is to "holy women" (3:5).

❖ *Search the Scriptures*

As last week's study showed, Peter was writing to believers scattered over the northern part of the province of Asia (modern-day Turkey). They were being persecuted because of their faith in Jesus Christ. Peter began his letter by reminding these believers that God has provided all the resources they need to live confidently. In this, the second section, he began to draw out the implications for everyday Christian living. Whereas the first 12 verses of the letter are filled with prayer and statements of fact, the next section turns to exhortation—urging these believers to "act right."

In this week's study the final item in each of the "lasting truths" sections identifies the main commands of the verses under study. They are called main commands based on the Greek grammatical structure of the passage.

Be Holy (1 Pet. 1:13-16)

*What was Peter picturing when he spoke of getting the mind ready for action? Why did he call believers **children**? Why did he connect Christian holiness to God's holiness?*

Verse 13: **Therefore, get your minds ready for action, being self-disciplined, and set your hope completely on the grace to be brought to you at the revelation of Jesus Christ.**

The little word **therefore** marks Peter's transition from declaration of truth to exhortation to action. The first item he mentioned was to **get your minds ready for action.** Literally, he said to "gird up the loins of your mind" (KJV). In a time when most people wore long garments, it was impossible to do any active physical work without tucking one's garments up into the belt or sash. Thus, those who had tucked in their garments were ready to work. Living the Christian life is a matter of focused, active attention. Another way to put this same truth is that of **being self-disciplined,** that is, to be alert and attentive to do what needs to be done, the opposite of being sleepy, drunk, or lazy.

The command **set your hope** is grammatically the most prominent in this verse. Peter had already stated the truth that believers have a "living hope" (v. 3). Now he asked them to live **completely** in the light of that hope, for there is no other sure hope. Here the hope is focused yet again on the final and complete state of **grace** that believers will experience when Christ returns at His **revelation.** Peter's readers had already begun to experience God's grace (v. 2); when Jesus returns His grace will overflow beyond anyone's present ability to grasp it.

***Verses 14-16:* As obedient children, do not be conformed to the desires of your former ignorance [15]but, as the One who called you is holy, you also are to be holy in all your conduct; [16]for it is written, Be holy, because I am holy."**

Peter called these Christians **obedient children,** not mainly because he thought of them in a fatherly and affectionate way. Rather, he knew that they had received the new birth from God (v. 3). This implies that they must behave in the way their Heavenly Father asked them to.

Before they were born again, while they were lost in sin, they had lived in **former ignorance**—what Peter later called an "empty way of life" (v. 18). Its characteristic was that of **desires** or self-centeredness. There was no choice then; Peter's readers (then and now) **conformed** to such selfishness because that is always the way of sin.

Now, however, there should be a change in **all your conduct.** The term **conduct** means lifestyle or way of living. Because believers have become part of a new family, they must continually become more like their Father in their attitudes and actions. One way they are to be like Him is to **be holy.** The **One who called** believers to a new life as part of His family **is holy,** that is, utterly set apart from sin. He always does what is right and pure, and He longs for His children to act right and pure as well. Thus, Christians are to act differently from the sinful culture that they live in. Jesus said that believers are "not of the world, just as I am not of the world" (John 17:14).

In 1 Peter 1:10-12, the apostle had made an important connection between the Old Testament prophets and the first-century fulfillment of their message (see last week's study). Now, for the first time in the letter, Peter quoted an Old Testament passage. In its original setting the passage connected God's holiness with His insistence that the Israelite people of the old covenant were to **be holy.** The same principle applies to Christian believers who are now part of Christ's new covenant. The God who had said **I am holy** to the Israelites was the same One who called the Christians to holy living.

Peter quoted the Book of Leviticus (11:44-45; 19:2), which is famous for teaching the Israelites that they were set apart (holy) to God and must participate in ceremonies of animal sacrifices and keep ritually clean. Because these requirements have been fulfilled by Christ's sacrifice, believers today express that they are set apart (holy) to God through becoming Christlike in their character.

What lasting truths are in these verses?

1. The Christian life is active, not passive, and requires self-discipline.

2. The Christian life means rejecting a lifestyle based on fulfilling selfish desires.

3. God's holiness is the basis for a believer's holiness.

4. The two main commands of this passage are "set your hope" and "be holy."

Be Loving (1 Pet 1:22-25)

*What is the relationship between obeying God and loving one another? What did Peter mean by **imperishable** seed? What is the relationship between the Word of God and the Christian gospel?*

Verses 22-23: By obedience to the truth, having purified yourselves for sincere love of the brothers, love one another earnestly from a pure heart, [23]since you have been born again—not of perishable seed but of imperishable—through the living and enduring word of God.

In the first part of verse 22, Peter affirmed two truths that he assumed his readers had experienced. He used these assumptions as a foundation for his next instruction. First, he noted that these Christians had experienced **obedience to the truth.** This did not mean that good works had saved them, but that when they heard the gospel preached, they had responded in the way that the gospel requires: repentance and faith. Second, Peter affirmed that God had **purified** them from their sins so that they had begun to have **sincere love of the brothers,** which refers to the natural affection brothers and sisters in the same family have for each other. Peter also wanted these believers to go beyond sincere natural affection. His command was to **love one another earnestly.** This time he used a verb form of the Greek noun *agape,* meaning a supernaturally given love for even the unlovable—a love that proves itself to the point of great sacrifice.

Peter knew that it is difficult, even impossible, to value people it is not natural for us to love. But Peter also knew that **a pure heart** will love. This is to say that someone with a heart purified through the forgiveness of sins will love others. Such a person loves because of God's love for him, someone unlovable. A person with such a heart has been **born again.** This is a supernatural love. People who have been born into God's family discover a God-given ability to love their (unlovable) brothers and sisters in the same family.

In the last part of verse 23 Peter expanded on the means through which believers are **born again.** He used human birth as an analogy. The conception and birth of human beings occurs when **perishable seed** is implanted. Perishable seed gives birth to a perishable life. Birth into God's family occurs when **imperishable** seed is implanted. Imperishable seed gives birth to an imperishable life. This seed is **the living and enduring word of God.**

Verses 24-25: **For**
"All flesh is like grass,
and all its glory like a flower of the grass.
The grass withers, and the flower drops off,
²⁵but the word of the Lord endures forever."
And this is the word that was preached as the gospel to you.

Just as in verse 16 Peter had based his exhortation to holiness on an Old Testament text, so now he used Scripture to uphold the contrast between that which is perishable (the merely human) and that which is permanent (God's Word). This time he went to the Book of Isaiah. God had revealed to Israel the temporary nature of human existence (Isa. 40:6-8). He had compared human existence to **grass.** When all is said and done, all the **glory** of human achievement is no more than **a flower of the grass**—here today and gone tomorrow.

Just as **grass withers,** just as **the flower drops off,** so it is with every purely human accomplishment.

What then may perishable humans latch onto that will last? Isaiah's answer was, **The word of the Lord endures forever.** If human beings want permanent success, then they will cling to what God has said will last forever. Peter had the same answer that Isaiah did, and he made it explicit for his readers. The heart of Scripture is **the gospel.** Those who have heard the good news **preached** have heard **the word** of God. The apostle Paul expressed the same principle this way: "So faith comes from what is heard, and what is heard comes through the message about Christ" (Rom. 10:17).

What lasting truths are in these verses?

1. God's Word is the agency through which humans are born again.
2. Everything merely human is as perishable as grass or flowers.
3. God's Word is living and imperishable.
4. The main command of this passage is "love one another earnestly."

Be Mature (1 Pet. 2:1-3)

What unholy behaviors did Peter ask the believers to turn away from? What image of maturing did he use? Did he use milk as a positive or a negative image? Why?

Verses 1-3: **So rid yourselves of all wickedness, all deceit, hypocrisy, envy, and all slander. ²Like newborn infants, desire the unadulterated spiritual milk, so that you may grow by it in your salvation, ³since "you have tasted that the Lord is good."**

In the last four verses of chapter 1, Peter used the image of birth. It was a logical development for Peter to continue the picture by thinking of a healthy, growing infant nursing at its mother's bosom. Before Peter developed this picture, however, he returned briefly to the principle that holiness means being set apart *from* sin as well as *to* God (see 1:14). He mentioned five unholy behaviors from which believers are to **rid** themselves—consciously and deliberately.

1. **Wickedness** is a general term for that which is morally evil. The rest of the list concerns specific kinds of wickedness. The qualifying term **all** is inclusive—no area of life is to escape our spiritual reflection.

2. **Deceit** refers to that which is fake or sham, especially in speech. Before conversion, people often pretend to be what they are not.

Afterward, integrity and sincerity are to become their hallmarks. Again, the **all** is inclusive.

3. **Hypocrisy** refers to playing a role in one's actions, or as we would say, being two-faced. In ancient times stage actors often wore masks, and this is where the Greek term used here originated. As believers grow in holiness, they stop play acting before other people.

4. **Envy** means wanting what someone else has. The last of the Ten Commandments prohibited this (Ex. 20:17). This mental sin can boil over into all sorts of open sins, such as theft, adultery, and murder. Holiness means that we grow in our contentment with God and His provisions for us (Phil. 4:11).

5. **Slander** is a word referring to evil speech directed at others. To cut down or smear another person has no place in the Christian's life. This can take many forms, but the **all** makes it quite inclusive.

One of the principles of science is that nature abhors a vacuum. This is true spiritually as well. When believers get rid of negative attitudes and behaviors, they must replace them with something positive lest they be filled with something more evil (see Matt. 12:43-45). Instead of drinking the poison of sin, believers can have **unadulterated** ("pure," NRSV) **spiritual milk.** By this Peter meant the Word of God taken into the believer's life (see 1 Pet. 1:23,25). It nourishes believers in their spiritual lives because it is **spiritual.** Other passages refer to milk as a negative image for immature believers who refuse to be weaned from it so they can eat solid food (see 1 Cor. 3:2; Heb. 5:12-13). But here Peter was using milk as an entirely positive picture. The milk of the Word of God is what nourishes us from the very moment we enter God's family.

After normal human birth comes nursing. After spiritual birth— being born again—believers are to **desire** God's Word **like newborn infants.** The Greek verb for **desire** is strong, meaning "to crave, to deeply long for." It stands as the main command of this passage. There is a kind of tension set up by Peter's use of the command form. On the one hand, once believers **have tasted that the Lord is good** they will surely keep coming back for more. Once someone has discovered the taste of honey, he or she knows where to go for something sweet. On the other hand, believers need to be reminded of where to go for nourishment. Unfortunately, there are cheap substitutes— spiritual "junk food"—that can replace the milk of the Word.

Peter's logic is like this. 1. Newly born-again believers have already tasted that God's Word is good since it was through God's Word that they were born again. 2. They are therefore to continue to take God's Word into their lives. 3. Those who take God's Word into their lives will **grow by it,** just as human infants who drink their mother's milk grow and mature.

Salvation begins with the new birth. There is more to it than that however. Salvation includes maturing and growing in holiness. Peter had heard Jesus teach, "Blessed are those who hunger and thirst for righteousness, because they will be filled" (Matt. 5:6). Those who earnestly desire to become more holy will become more holy—as long as they feast on God's provisions.

Verse 3 is the third of Peter's Old Testament quotations in this study, this one from Psalm 34:8. Again, his use of Scripture stresses the principles shared between Old Testament saints and New Testament believers. Abraham, David, and God's people before Christ's coming experienced the goodness of God through receiving His message into their lives. Throughout the Old Testament, but especially in the Psalms, exuberant expressions about the wonders of God's Word abound. The greatest expression of this is Psalm 119, an extensive meditation on God's Word revealed to His people. The need and desire for God's Word continues to be true for those who live after Christ's death and resurrection.

What lasting truths are in these verses?

1. Evil attitudes, speech, and behavior have no place in the life of a believer.

2. A healthy baby nurtured from its mother's milk is a good picture of Christian growth.

3. All true believers have already experienced the goodness of God in His Word.

4. The main command of this passage is "desire . . . unadulterated spiritual milk."

Be Honorable (1 Pet. 2:11-12)

*What did Peter mean by honorable conduct? What conflicts between believers and a secular society did Peter envision? What does **day of visitation** refer to?*

Verses 11-12: Dear friends, I urge you as aliens and temporary residents to abstain from fleshly desires that war against you. ¹²Conduct yourselves honorably among the Gentiles, so that in a

case where they speak against you as those who do evil, they may, by observing your good works, glorify God in a day of visitation.

These two verses show the permanent tension under which Christians carry out their lives as saints. Here is another great reminder from Peter that success—from God's point of view—is utterly different from the world's view of success. The right actions that God expects from His people will cause clashes with those who are not His people. Note the following points of tension.

1. *The tension of identity:* **dear friends** versus **aliens and temporary residents.** These believers were so well known to Peter (and to God) that they were **dear friends** (literally, "beloved"). They were secure in this status. Yet they should remember that the world was not their final destination. In the first verse of his letter, Peter had called them "temporary residents," and he reminded them of this again here. As wonderful as the imagery of home is, we are to remember that there is a truer, better home waiting for us in heaven.

2. *The tension of desires:* the spiritual desire to **abstain from fleshly desires** versus indulging in them. Those born again desire to please God and find their satisfaction in Him. But they have not yet lost their capacity to desire wrong things. The flesh, that which is centered in the sinful self, is at **war against** the true spiritual self—**you,** literally, "the soul" (see Rom. 7:13-25).

3. *The tension of reputation:* to **conduct yourselves honorably** versus being spoken of as **those who do evil.** In 1 Peter 1:15 the apostle had urged believers to be holy in "all your conduct" or lifestyle. Now he used the same word again, this time using the modifier **honorably** instead of "holy." The two are parallel. Holy conduct is honorable, good, decent behavior—a life lived in the light of eternity and in the light of the holiness of God. Such a lifestyle never makes sense to **the Gentiles,** who live only for the here and now. Therefore, they will **speak against** believers because they misunderstand both their motives and their actions. Throughout Scripture the pattern is that God's people are often maligned by the world. Peter may have been thinking of Jesus' teaching: "Blessed are you when they insult you and persecute you, and say every kind of evil against you falsely because of Me" (Matt. 5:11).

4. *The tension of coming judgment:* **good works** now versus a **day of visitation** later. Unbelievers are constantly **observing** the **good works** of Christians even while they are maligning them, and they will one day **glorify God.** One day every tongue will "confess that Jesus

Christ is Lord, to the glory of God the Father" (Phil. 2:11). The **day of visitation** could refer either to the time that God comes in *mercy*, visiting a sinful Gentile with salvation through hearing and responding to the gospel, or to the time when God comes in *wrath*, visiting a sinful Gentile with punishment—either in this lifetime or at the final judgment. In either case, Christians are called on to remember that they have a responsibility to live **honorably** so that unbelievers will **glorify God** in some way.

What lasting truths are in these verses?

1. Fleshly desires wage war against believers throughout life.

2. Holy, honorable conduct is often observed and misunderstood by unbelievers.

3. An honorable lifestyle brings glory to God.

4. The main command of this passage is, "I urge you . . . to abstain from fleshly desires."

❖ Spiritual Transformations

The *Life Question* this lesson seeks to address is, How should I act as a Christian? Peter has shown the way by his strong encouragement to early believers concerning their lifestyles. In two words he told them, "Be holy." How does this happen? Believers succeed in acting right—being holy—as they follow the essential commands Peter gave them:

"Set your hope completely on the grace to be brought to you" (1:13).

"Be holy in all your conduct" (1:15).

"Love one another earnestly from a pure heart" (1:22).

"Desire the unadulterated spiritual milk" (2:2).

"Abstain from fleshly desires" (2:11).

Which of the commands listed above do you need to work on the most? Why? _____

_____

Whom do you know that you might encourage with the message in this study? What will you say to this person? _____

_____

Prayer of Commitment: *Dear God, Thank You for Peter's strong teaching on holy living. Infuse Your Word into my life so that I am marked by holiness, love, maturity, and honor. Amen.*

Week of August 22

BE HUMBLE

Background Passages: 1 Peter 2:13–3:12; 5:5-7
Focal Passages: 1 Peter 2:13-14,17-21; 3:1-4,7-9; 5:5-7
Key Verse: 1 Peter 2:21

❖ *Significance of the Lesson*

• The *Theme* of this lesson is that successful living includes practicing humility.
• The *Life Question* this lesson seeks to address is, How should I demonstrate humility?
• The *Biblical Truth* is that humility, which includes having a proper perspective of one's responsibilities toward God and toward others, is an essential ingredient for living a successful and fulfilled life.
• The *Life Impact* is to help you live humbly.

How Is Success Related to Being Humble?

"It's hard to be humble when you're as great as I am."

Such a statement produces a chuckle or wry smile. Nobody likes arrogant, proud people, yet today's society generally encourages individuals to focus on themselves and on their own desires. Meeting the needs of others doesn't rate very high on the "Success Meter." God has a different understanding. Believers who show genuine humility will stand out. As they act in the best interest of others they will be conspicuous, because from a merely human perspective this means they are doing something that doesn't come naturally. Success as God defines it involves relying on Him to exercise true humility—including having a proper perspective on one's responsibilities both to others and to God.

Word Study: *Humble, humility* (1 Pet. 5:5,6)

The Greek word for **humble** is part of a word family that indicates something is of lowly character or status. In Greek society, this word family generally had negative implications. A culture valuing strength and self-sufficiency considered lowliness to be weakness, even a vice. Jesus changed that by affirming, "I am gentle and humble in heart" (Matt. 11:29). He taught that all who humble themselves will be rewarded (Matt. 23:12; Luke 14:11; 18:14). Humility is the opposite of putting self first; rather, it means putting the needs of others first. God has promised grace to those who practice such humility (Jas. 4:6; 1 Pet. 5:5).

❖ *Search the Scriptures*

As we have seen, Peter wrote to persecuted believers scattered over the northern part of the province of Asia (modern-day Turkey). Peter began his letter by reminding these Christians that God has provided all the resources they need to live confidently as believers. In the second section, he drew out the implications for everyday Christian living, urging these believers to act right by being holy. This week's study, drawn mainly from verses in the center section, focuses on human relationships and how humility in these relationships is essential for living a successful and fulfilled life as God defines it.

Submit to Authorities (1 Pet. 2:13-14,17-19)

How inclusive was Peter's command for Christians to submit to authorities? What functions did Peter envision for the government of his day? Why were Christian slaves asked to submit to their owners?

Verses 13-14: Submit to every human institution because of the Lord, whether to the Emperor as the supreme authority, [14]or to governors as those sent out by him to punish those who do evil and to praise those who do good.

One of the great universal principles is that of authority and recognition of that authority. Relationships in every sphere of life depend on acknowledging proper authorities. This is true in government, education, business, families, and churches. Believers, like everyone else, must understand and follow this principle.

The Christians Peter addressed probably had questions about how—or even whether—to submit to secular Roman authorities. He assured them that this was the right thing to do, but he gave good reasons for his instructions. The Greek word for **submit** is strong, meaning "yield, be subject to, be under an authority." When people submit, it does not mean that they are inherently inferior; rather it has to do with accepting a role for the sake of order. As we will see, Peter was fond of using this particular verb in his letter.

Peter was thinking of submission to **every human institution.** In the context, he was referring to governmental authorities, as the references to **the Emperor** and **governors** show. Peter's foundation for this command was simple but profound: **because of the Lord.** God has set in place the mechanisms by which governments—as sinful or as inefficient as they may be—exist. Believers are to recognize this and submit to them, even when **the supreme authority** is not noted for justice. In fact, the Emperor at this time was the infamous Nero.

The submission that Peter commanded does not include actions contrary to God's will. Whenever human authorities conflict with God's commands, believers are to submit to God. Many years earlier, Peter had said, "We must obey God rather than men" (Acts 5:29).

Peter gave a second reason for submission. The Lord has designated government authorities **to punish those who do evil and to praise those who do good.** Around the world and throughout human history, restraining evildoers and bringing them to justice has been recognized as one of the primary purposes of government. Because of this function, believers are certainly allowed to be involved in government or to seek to persuade those in authority to become more effective in doing what is right. Biblical submission does not prohibit believers from speaking out against immoral policies promoted by those in authority. Peter would have agreed that believers have a responsibility respectfully to urge those in authority to promote policies that are consistent with God's values as revealed in Scripture.

Verses 17-19: **Honor everyone. Love the brotherhood. Fear God. Honor the Emperor.**

[18]Household slaves, submit yourselves to your masters with all respect, not only to the good and gentle but also to the cruel. [19]For it brings favor if, because of conscience toward God, someone endures grief from suffering unjustly.

Verse 17 shows that diverse relationships are to be treated differently. The general command is to **honor everyone.** Each human being is made in the image of God and therefore is to be respected. In the case of those in **the brotherhood,** that is, the family of brothers and sisters in the body of Christ, honor is best shown by **love.** Scripture emphasizes many times the importance of mutual love among Christians.

The honor due to God by Christians is to **fear** Him. Earlier in his letter, Peter had reminded his readers to "conduct yourselves in reverence [fear] during this time of temporary residence" (1:17). Believers do not cringe in terror before God; rather, they respect and revere Him, for this is the foundation for holy living (see also Prov. 1:7; 8:13).

Interestingly, Peter used the same verb for **honor** to describe the believer's respect for **the Emperor** that he did for **everyone.** People in government are also human beings and are not qualitatively different from any other person. Believers submit to them because of their function, not because they are somehow innately superior beings.

In the first century, wealthy homes had **household slaves.** Some had become believers. Peter now applied the principle of submission to them. They were to **submit** to their **masters** just as all believers were to submit to authorities. They owed **all respect** (a noun form of the verb translated **fear** in v. 17) to their masters because of the master's authority role and because they too were made in God's image. This was true whether masters were **good and gentle** or whether they were **cruel.** Thankfully, slaves no longer exist in our society, but the principle applies to the employee-employer relationship. Whether bosses are respectable or not, Christians owe them respect.

Verse 19 gives another reason for submission in the workplace. Here is Peter's argument. First, Christians with a **conscience toward God** submit even to unrespectable bosses because they accept the God-given principle of submission. Second, sometimes these Christians endure **grief,** even **suffering unjustly** in the workplace. Third, such unjust suffering brings **favor** (the word is usually translated "grace") from God—and Christians then have the joy of experiencing the grace of God afresh.

What lasting truths are in these verses?

1. One function of government is to punish evil and to praise good.

2. God wants Christians to submit to their government unless actions contrary to His will are demanded.

3. God wants Christian employees to submit to their bosses unless actions contrary to His will are demanded.

4. God gives special grace to those who suffer unjustly.

Imitate Christ (1 Pet 2:20-21)

What is the wrong way to suffer? How is experiencing unjust suffering Christlike? What does it mean to follow in Christ's footsteps?

Verses 20-21: **For what credit is there if you endure when you sin and are beaten? But when you do good and suffer, if you endure, it brings favor with God.**
²¹For you were called to this,
because Christ also suffered for you,
leaving you an example,
so that you should follow in His steps.

In the original context, Peter was still thinking of Christian slaves who might be mistreated or even physically **beaten** by cruel masters. The principle, however, is much broader and applies to all believers who have faced an unfair situation—from family, in school, at work, in the neighborhood, or elsewhere.

On the one hand, there are situations (of **sin**) in which punishment (being **beaten**) is deserved. No spiritual **credit** is given for a Christian to **endure** this, although sad to say this does happen. On the other hand, there are circumstances (doing **good**) in which punishment (being made to **suffer**) is undeserved. God sees and cares. He desires that His children **endure** this. In fact, it is a sign of **favor with God** to face unjust suffering!

At first, this line of reasoning sounds backward. Yet Peter pressed the point by noting that this is one of the ways God has of making us more like Jesus. He affirmed that believers have been **called to this** unjust suffering. This is no accident or failure on God's part; rather, God desires for His redeemed children to share in some of the same experiences that His Son endured. First, however, Peter made it clear that in some ways the suffering of Christians was *unlike* the suffering of Jesus. When He suffered and died, He was the substitute **for** sinners—something only He could do (Isa. 53:6).

But Jesus' suffering was also the greatest example in history of enduring evil in return for doing good. He was a prototype for His followers to have as **an example.** Thus, when believers **follow in His steps,** it is a great privilege they receive of being so much *like* Jesus in His sufferings. The testimony of multiplied thousands of persecuted believers throughout church history is that they have counted this as an honor. Peter himself was involved in one of the first such beatings, and "they went out . . . rejoicing that they were counted worthy to be dishonored on behalf of the name" (Acts 5:41). Following Him has never been without risks, but identifying with Jesus and His sufferings should also be considered a privilege by those who know Him.

What lasting truths are in these verses?

1. For Christians it is a privilege to endure unjust suffering.

2. Christ's experience of unjust suffering is an example for believers to follow.

Honor Your Spouse (1 Pet. 3:1-4,7)

What kind beauty does God desire from Christian women? Why is it right for a Christian wife to submit to her husband? What responsibilities does a Christian husband have to his wife?

Verses 1-4: Wives, in the same way, submit yourselves to your own husbands so that, even if some disobey the Christian message, they may be won over without a message by the way their wives live, ²when they observe your pure, reverent lives. ³Your beauty should not consist of outward things like elaborate hairstyles and the wearing of gold ornaments or fine clothes; ⁴instead, it should consist of the hidden person of the heart with the imperishable quality of a gentle and quiet spirit, which is very valuable in God's eyes.

Every religion should be concerned with the impact it has on the husband and wife relationship. When Christians follow the principles Peter outlined here, they find marriage and family life strengthened; indeed, wherever the gospel message has been embraced and applied, great benefits to family life have appeared.

In the same way indicates that the principle of authority in government and the workplace also applies in marriage. The verb **submit** is the same and does not mean that wives are less intelligent or less valuable than their husbands. It does not mean that a Christian wife must do all the giving or that she cannot express her thoughts. It does mean that the wife should accept her role in marriage and yield to her husband for the sake of order. Peter gave two reasons for Christian wives to do this.

First, unbelieving husbands (those who **disobey the Christian message**) may be **won over** to Christ **by the way their wives live.** Christian wives who live **pure, reverent lives** ("chaste conduct accompanied by fear," NKJV) will not need to nag their husbands. A Christ-centered life is a powerful testimony to the truth of the gospel.

Second, living as a godly wife **is very valuable in God's eyes.** All Christians want to grow in their love for God. Christian wives can express their love to Him by their lifestyles. Peter said that God values character more than external appearances. **Elaborate hairstyles and . . . gold ornaments or fine clothes** are not what give a Christian woman true **beauty.** Rather, the Christlike character **hidden** beneath the surface is more important. **A gentle and quiet spirit** lasts for eternity; all that is material fades quickly. Peter was not forbidding Christian women from being well groomed or nicely dressed. He was emphasizing what a wife's priority should be.

Verse 7: **Husbands, in the same way, live with your wives with understanding of their weaker nature yet showing them honor as co-heirs of the grace of life, so that your prayers will not be hindered.**

Christian **husbands** are to understand and live by the principle of authority and submission **in the same way** that Christian wives do. Peter mentioned two factors that husbands must never forget in their marriage.

First, there is no question that in general women have a **weaker nature** than men do. This simply means that typically women have less physical strength than men. (A more literal translation is "weaker vessel"; KJV). Morally and spiritually, of course, women are often much stronger than their husbands. Rare is the marriage, however, in which the woman physically has more strength or stamina, and this is a fact of earthly existence. Males can forget this; therefore, they are called on to **live . . . with understanding** that their wives should be treated with care.

Second, Christian wives are **co-heirs of the grace of life.** They experience full salvation—just as much as men do. They will live in resurrected, perfect bodies in heaven forever—just as much as men will. Christian husbands therefore should **honor** their wives as individuals created in God's image and redeemed for eternal salvation. Husbands who forget this will be ineffective in their spiritual lives. Those who keep it in mind discover that their **prayers will not be hindered.**

What lasting truths are in these verses?

1. Christian wives honor their husbands by submitting to them.

2. Christian husbands honor their wives by living with them in light of both time (their physical weaknesses) and eternity (their sharing in full salvation).

Show Compassion (1 Pet. 3:8-9)

*What contrasts did Peter have in mind when he wrote about Christian compassion? What does it mean to give someone a **blessing**?*

Verses 8-9: **Now finally, all of you should be like-minded and sympathetic, should love believers, and be compassionate and humble, ⁹not paying back evil for evil or insult for insult but, on the contrary, giving a blessing, since you were called for this, so that you can inherit a blessing.**

The section of Peter's letter from 2:13 through 3:7 focuses on the topic of humble submission to authorities in three dimensions of life: government, the workplace, and marriage. In these verses the apostle provided a wrap-up to the general topic, as indicated by the word **finally.** He was writing to **all of you,** whether a government authority or a citizen; whether a master or a slave; whether a husband or a wife. All believers are to demonstrate the following positive characteristics in whatever arena of life they are facing. Being **like-minded** refers to thinking together or harmoniously with others, or at least as much as possible (see Rom. 12:18). **Sympathetic** means having mutual feelings with others, especially sharing sorrow. **Love believers** refers to having family-like affections for others in the body of Christ. **Compassionate** refers to feeling others' needs and then acting to meet those needs. **Humble** refers to lowliness of mind or attitude that keeps a person from being puffed up or consumed with concerns and desires about self.

In contrast to these attitudes are those that me-first people exhibit. The natural tendency is to get even with others for their *deeds* **(paying back evil for evil)** or for their *words* **(insult for insult).** Perhaps Peter was recalling Jesus' teaching in the Sermon on the Mount: "I tell you, don't resist an evildoer. On the contrary, if anyone slaps you on your right cheek, turn the other to him also" (Matt. 5:39).

Instead of retaliating, Peter said that Christians were to give a **blessing.** Blessing is the opposite of cursing (wishing ill on someone). Jesus had explained this also in the Sermon on the Mount: "Love your enemies, and pray for those who persecute you, so that you may be sons of your Father in heaven" (Matt. 5:44-45; see Rom. 12:17-20). The best way to deal with enemies is to pray for them and perhaps to lead them to Christ.

God has **called** His people into certain situations so that they can be **giving a blessing** to others in this lifetime. Those who do so, especially by forgiving the unforgiving or blessing those who curse them, are giving evidence that they have received God's forgiveness and will one day **inherit a blessing**—eternity with God.

What lasting truths are in these verses?

1. Christians are to get along with others but then to act on behalf of others as well.

2. Christians are to be a blessing to others rather than a burden.

Depend on God (1 Pet. 5:5-7)

What relationships within a church's life are included in humility? What does it mean for someone to cast his or her cares on God?

Verses 5-7: Likewise, you younger men, be subject to the elders. And all of you clothe yourselves with humility toward one another, because

"God resists the proud,

but gives grace to the humble."

⁶Humble yourselves therefore under the mighty hand of God, so that He may exalt you in due time, ⁷casting all your care upon Him, because He cares about you.

In 1 Peter 4, one of the main themes is suffering as a Christian (see next week's study). In 1 Peter 5, the apostle was concerned with relationships in the church. He returned to the principle of authority and submission that he had earlier developed. The same Greek verb translated "submit" in 2:13 is now rendered **be subject.** God has placed spiritual leaders called **elders** in the church to provide order and guidance. Others are called on to recognize this. Peter may have singled out the **younger men** because they are the ones most likely to resist such authority.

At the same time, everyone in the body of Christ—leaders and followers alike—are to act **with humility toward one another.** Peter quoted Proverbs 3:34 (see also Jas. 4:6), which says that God opposes those who are **proud** or arrogant and that those who deliberately choose to be **humble** will be the special recipients of His **grace.**

The climax and conclusion of this study is found in verses 6-7. Every believer has relationships in this life in which the principle of authority and submission is ongoing: government, workplace, marriage, and church. Yet there is another overarching relationship where the same principle is at work—the relationship with God Himself. When believers have first humbled themselves **under the mighty hand of God,** they will have no difficulty being humble within various human relationships in this life. Why? Because God has promised to **exalt** such humble believers **in due time.** Perhaps this will happen in this lifetime, but probably not. Certainly, however, it will happen in heaven. Jesus said, "Everyone who exalts himself will be humbled, and the one who humbles himself will be exalted" (Luke 14:11).

Because this promise from God is sure, believers can have confidence in **casting all** their **care upon Him**—including the times that they have obediently submitted to authority and things have become difficult. Believers are to be in no doubt that **He cares about** them, no matter what the circumstances. Just as God exalted His Son after He suffered unjustly, so He will exalt His other children.

What lasting truths are in these verses?

1. Christians are to relate to each other in humility.
2. Christians are to humble themselves before God.
3. God has promised to care for and exalt those who depend on Him.

❖ *Spiritual Transformations*

The *Life Question* this lesson seeks to address is, How should I demonstrate humility? The answer is first of all to be found in humbly submitting to God. Second, however, is the matter of having a proper perspective about one's relationship with others. This includes living according to the principle of authority and submission in a variety of realms: government, the workplace, marriage, and church. God has promised to care for—and ultimately exalt—those who live in humility.

Whom do you know that may be confused about the issue of humility and submission and with whom you might share this message? How can you help that person? _____

_____

In which area of your life do you find the most difficulty expressing humility or submission? _____

_____

What can you do during the coming week to demonstrate your willingness to live more humbly? _____

_____

Prayer of Commitment: *Dear Heavenly Father, Help me first of all to humble myself under Your hand, knowing that You really care for me. Show me how to live in relationships that honor Your principles of authority and submission. Amen.*

TAKE COURAGE

Background Passages: 1 Peter 3:13–4:6,12-19
Focal Passages: 1 Peter 3:13-17; 4:1-3,12-16,19
Key Verse: 1 Peter 3:15

❖ *Significance of the Lesson*

• The *Theme* of this lesson is that successful living includes faithfulness and courage in the midst of suffering.
• The *Life Question* this lesson seeks to address is, How can I show faithfulness and courage, even when my allegiance to Christ is ridiculed?
• The *Biblical Truth* is that God enables believers to stand faithfully and courageously for Him, even when their allegiance to Christ is ridiculed.
• The *Life Impact* is to help you show faithfulness and courage in your allegiance to Christ.

How Is Success Related to Taking Courage?

"I believe we should affirm all religious views and moral systems. I'm a tolerant person."

"You Christians are so narrow minded when it comes to certain spiritual and moral truths. I can't accept your view as a valid position when there are so many other views out there to consider."

There is both irony and tragedy in these two statements, both of which are becoming more and more popular in contemporary culture. People seem to want to tolerate all views *except* for those that are strongly committed to absolute truth. Every day moral relativism clashes further with Christianity, and the biblical worldview is increasingly misunderstood, ridiculed, and rejected. For the Apostle Peter, success was not found by being accepted by the culture of his day. Success was found by living in faithfulness and courage amid persecution or rejection. Successful Christians are those who adhere to God's values in terms of what they believe and how they live.

Word Study: *Ridiculed* (1 Pet. 4:14)

The Greek verb *oneidizo* means "to ridicule" and occurs nine times in the New Testament (for example, Matt. 5:11; 11:20; 27:44; Rom. 15:3; 1 Pet. 4:14). The related noun *oneidismos* ("ridicule") occurs five times (Rom. 15:3; 1 Tim. 3:7; Heb. 10:33; 11:26; 13:13). Speaking aloud against someone or something, sometimes justly but usually unjustly, is the essential idea of both words. English terms such as *insult* and *revile* are close synonyms.

Jesus denounced *(oneidizo)* the unrepentant citizens of Chorazin, Bethsaida, and Capernaum (Matt. 11:20). By contrast, Jesus Himself was the object of unjust ridicule at His trial and crucifixion (Mark 15:32). He taught His disciples that God would bless them when they were insulted for His sake (Matt. 5:11; Luke 6:22). The writers of the epistles continued this teaching by asking believers to endure ridicule with joy for Christ's sake (Heb. 10:33-34; 1 Pet. 4:13-14). Moses is a good Old Testament example of a righteous person who "considered reproach for the sake of the Messiah to be greater wealth than the treasures of Egypt, since his attention was on the reward" (Heb. 11:26).

❖ *Search the Scriptures*

First Peter was addressed to believers scattered over the northern part of the province of Asia (modern-day Turkey). This is our fourth and final study on this letter. In every chapter he mentioned suffering directly, either by Christ or by Christians. In this study the emphasis is on selected texts in chapters 3 and 4 in which Peter focused on the need to remain courageous and strong. This is true especially when believers face opposition to the gospel or ridicule because of their allegiance to Christ. Peter addressed Christians' suffering in the first century, so the increasing intolerance of today's society against Christ is nothing new. Those who resolve to be faithful to Him are joining multiplied thousands of other believers from many centuries and from many lands.

Be Ready to Defend Your Faith (1 Pet. 3:13-17)

What kinds of suffering did Peter expect that his readers would experience? What actions should suffering saints expect to take? What attitudes should suffering saints seek to maintain?

Verses 13-15: **And who will harm you if you are passionate for what is good?** [14]**But even if you should suffer for righteousness, you are blessed. "Do not fear what they fear or be disturbed,"** [15]**but set apart the Messiah as Lord in your hearts, and always be ready to give a defense to anyone who asks you for a reason for the hope that is in you.**

Even the most irreligious people recognize **what is good** when they see it. In general, acts of kindness and concern for others are praised, not condemned. Thus, the answer to the question **who will harm you if you are passionate for what is good?** is "nobody." Particularly when Christians **are passionate** or enthusiastic about doing the right thing, others in society acknowledge their good deeds even if they do not embrace their God. Just think about how many hospitals, orphanages, schools, and other wonderful institutions have been founded by Christian people all over the world—often in countries that officially oppose open proclamation of the gospel. Furthermore, Christian groups are well regarded for being at the forefront of disaster relief.

On occasion Christians **suffer for righteousness.** In the Greek text the grammatical construction for **even if** states a condition unlikely to occur. When it does happen, however, God promises a special blessing (Matt. 5:10-12). Peter knew that the usual human response in such a situation is to be afraid of those who caused their suffering. He recalled the prophet Isaiah's words and quoted from Isaiah 8:12, which says that God's people are not to **fear** as if they were unbelievers who become fearful and **disturbed** as they face difficulties.

Isaiah reminded the Israelites of his day that the Lord is holy and only He is to be feared (v. 13). Peter applied Isaiah's principle by reminding his Christian readers that they were to **set apart the Messiah as Lord,** that is, to fear and respect Him *inwardly.* They were not to doubt Him if suffering for righteousness' sake occurred.

Peter also told believers to **be ready** to do something *outwardly:* **to give a defense to anyone who asks.** The word translated **defense** is *apologia,* the basis of the English term *apologetics.* This term relates to making a careful, reasoned case for the truth of something, such as might be done in a courtroom. As used by Christians, it refers to showing reasons for believing Christianity is true. (The term *apologetics* carries none of the negative undertones of the English term *apology.*) Believers are to give focused attention to the matter of knowing the **reason for the hope that is in** them.

We Christians should prepare to share our faith, whether or not we are actively suffering for Christ. We will not have good answers to give to unbelievers without preparation. During the past few years a number of outstanding resources have appeared in print to help us learn Christian apologetics. These include Paul Little's *Know Why You Believe* (Downers Grove,IL: InterVarsity, 2000); Josh McDowell's *The New Evidence that Demands a Verdict* (Nashville,TN: Thomas Nelson, 1999); and Lee Strobel's *The Case for Faith* (Grand Rapids,MI: Zondervan, 2000).

***Verses 16-17:* However, do this with gentleness and respect, keeping your conscience clear, so that when you are accused, those who denounce your Christian life will be put to shame. [17]For it is better to suffer for doing good, if that should be God's will, than for doing evil.**

Last week's study developed the theme of humility in relationships. When Christians have occasion to defend or share their faith, this same attitude is necessary. As Christians become more confident that they are equipped with the truth, it is possible for them to share the truth arrogantly or harshly. A strong gospel presentation should be made **with gentleness** and with **respect** (literally "fear") toward those who are listening.

Another essential part of the defense of the gospel is the credibility of the believer's lifestyle. Christians do not have to achieve moral perfection before they can share their faith, but they must strive to keep their **conscience clear.** Unbelievers will consider those with open sin in their lives to be fakes. They will **denounce** people like this, and such Christians **will be put to shame**—and deservedly so.

When Christians **suffer for doing good,** they can be sure that it is **God's will.** He plans such occasions in the lives of believers for His glory and for the believer's good. As Peter had just noted, suffering for doing good things can often become an occasion for sharing the gospel and perhaps leading a persecutor to Christ. But if Christians **suffer . . . for doing evil,** they should become ashamed and repent. Their repentance would make them regret that that their actions have spoiled an opportunity to witness for Christ.

What lasting truths are in these verses?

1. Believers are to be passionate about doing deeds of kindness and goodness.

2. When Christians suffer for righteousness, this is a great opportunity to share their faith.

3. Presenting the gospel properly means being gentle with and showing respect for unbelievers.

Remember Christ's Example (1 Pet 4:1-3)

Why did Peter connect the believer's suffering and Christ's suffering? What sinful activities did Peter ask believers to leave behind?

Verses 1-3: Therefore, since Christ suffered in the flesh, arm yourselves also with the same resolve—because the One who suffered in the flesh has finished with sin— ²in order to live the remaining time in the flesh, no longer for human desires, but for God's will. ³For there has already been enough time spent in doing the will of the pagans: carrying on in unrestrained behavior, evil desires, drunkenness, orgies, carousing, and lawless idolatry.

In 1 Peter 3:18-22 Peter described how **Christ suffered in the flesh,** that is, during the time of His life on earth. As noted in last week's discussion of 2:20, Christ's suffering and death were in many ways *unlike* the believer's suffering. Yet in other ways the two suffering are *alike.* **With the same resolve** that Jesus faced suffering, so should believers face suffering.

Peter's next statement is difficult to understand: **the One who suffered in the flesh has finished with sin.** If **the One** is a reference to Jesus, then Peter was pointing to Jesus' suffering on the cross as the way of being **finished with sin** by paying its price. If the reference is to a suffering believer (which the grammar permits), then it implies the following: By their willingness to suffer for righteousness, Christian sufferers show that they have made a break with the old sinful way of life described in verses 2-3. "A Christian does not, through suffering, magically vault the level of moral perfection. Verses 1-2 indicate that believers take seriously their struggle against sin and their commitment to obedience. By following this counsel, you demonstrate to others that obeying God is the most important motivation for your life, more important by far than avoiding hardship and pain."[1]

Christ's entire life and ministry showed what it means to live not **for human desires, but for God's will** (see Luke 22:42). When believers by suffering or by some other means come to the point in their lives that they want to do everything according to **God's will,** then they will be eager **to live the remaining time in the flesh** (during the rest of their lives on earth) for God, not for self.

Peter's original readers probably had been **pagans** (Gentiles worshiping many idols) before they were Christians. There had **already been
enough time spent** living an immoral lifestyle. From now on, they were
to concentrate on following Christ's example of living **for God's will.**
Peter was particularly concerned to warn these Christians about not
slipping back into certain activities associated with their previous lives,
and he mentioned several of them. **Unrestrained behavior** is shameless
sexual behavior, debauchery, and lewdness. **Evil desires** renders the
word traditionally translated "lusts." It referred especially to the sexual
appetite, but was not limited to sexual matters. **Drunkenness** is self-
explanatory. In our time, the use of illegal drugs (or misuse of pre-
scription drugs) would surely be included. **Orgies** of course means wild
sexual parties. Paul connected alcohol with illicit sex in Romans 13:13
and Galatians 5:21. The Greek word for **carousing** occurs here only in
the New Testament, but there is little doubt that it means just what
the English translation suggests—loose and wild living. **Lawless idolatry** refers to the worship of anything other than the true God—another
indication that the original readers were primarily Gentiles.

What lasting truths are in these verses?

1. Christ's suffering is a model for Christians when they suffer.

2. A believer's time on earth should be spent doing God's will.

3. The will of God never includes the typically immoral behaviors
of pagans.

Count It a Privilege to Suffer for Christ (1 Pet. 4:12-16)

*How can Christ's followers prepare to face suffering? What positive
terms did Peter use to discuss persecution? What was unusual about
using the term **Christian** in this passage?*

**Verses 12-13: Dear friends, when the fiery ordeal arises among
you to test you, don't be surprised by it, as if something unusual
were happening to you. [13]Instead, as you share in the sufferings of
the Messiah rejoice, so that you may also rejoice with great joy at
the revelation of His glory.**

Peter knew the readers of his letter well enough to call them **dear
friends** (literally "beloved"), something he had already done at 2:11.
This was, however, the first occasion in which he had called their
experiences of persecution a **fiery ordeal,** literally, "the burning"—a
reference to the severity and pain caused by the event. (Anyone who

has lost a home due to fire can attest to how devastating such an experience can be.) Christians should not **be surprised** when they go through these times. It was not **unusual** for believers to face hostility to the point of great pain and loss, and it is quite common today. In fact, Christian historians have agreed that more Christians were martyred in the twentieth century than in any other century.

In his life as an apostle, Peter had changed and grown dramatically. Early on he had rejected entirely the idea of **the sufferings of the Messiah** (Matt. 16:21-23). He had seen this happen before his eyes, however, and came to understand that this was God's plan for His Son (Acts 2:23). Now he further accepted that God's plan was that sometimes believers **share in the sufferings of** Jesus, that is, they follow His example.

What purpose does God have in mind? In general, He uses suffering **to test** believers so that their faith will grow. As believers realize this truth, they will **rejoice** even as they go through the test. Jesus "for the joy that lay before Him endured a cross and despised the shame" (Heb. 12:2). It should be no surprise that God plans for His other children to go through suffering on the way to **glory.**

Jesus had joy in suffering in light of His ultimate exaltation. He "despised the shame, and has sat down at the right hand of God's throne" (Heb. 12:2). So it is with Christian joy in suffering now. It happens in light of their coming final exaltation, the time when they will **rejoice with great joy at the revelation of His glory.**

Many people in society live as if the avoidance of pain is their main goal in life. Who knows how many billions of dollars are spent annually on pain relief? (And there is nothing wrong with taking aspirin for a headache!) Yet in God's plan the pain of persecution is a means to **great joy.** Although pain for its own sake is evil, pain as a means to joy (as in labor pains that result in the birth of a child) is a great good.

***Verses 14-16:* If you are ridiculed for the name of Christ, you are blessed, because the Spirit of glory and of God rests on you. [15]None of you, however, should suffer as a murderer, a thief, an evildoer, or as a meddler. [16]But if anyone suffers as a Christian, he should not be ashamed, but should glorify God with that name.**

No Christian should go out looking for persecution and suffering. In His loving sovereignty God will send it at the time and place of His choosing. It may come in the form of being verbally **ridiculed for the name of Christ.** When believers are insulted in this way, they

are blessed by God. He is fulfilling His plan for their lives. They should take such ridicule as a sign for both the present and for the future. *In the present*, ridicule is evidence that **the Spirit . . . of God rests** on them. It's as if Peter were saying, "Do you want to know that the Holy Spirit is at work in you? You'll have all the proof you want as soon as persecution comes into your life." Ridicule is also evidence of something that will happen *in the future:* **the Spirit of glory** will assure the believers that at the revelation of Christ's glory they too will share His glory. Suffering never means that God has failed. Far from it. Suffering is a triumph of God's purposes in the believer's life both for time and for eternity.

Readers of the *King James Version* may note that verse 14 ends with the following phrase omitted in most contemporary translations: "on their part he is evil spoken of, but on your part he is glorified." The sense is that persecutors are speaking evil of Christ while the believers are praising Him. Although the best manuscripts of 1 Peter do not have this phrase, Peter would have agreed with the truth it expresses even though he did not write it.

As we have seen already, Peter was aware of the possibility that professing Christians would do evil and then suffer the consequences (3:17). In 4:15 he returned briefly to that theme, this time noting specific evil deeds that ought to result in punishment. No just society can operate without giving criminals their deserved penalty. Four such criminals are noted.

A murderer is rightly condemned by all. Part of the government's responsibility is to see to it that murderers get what they deserve. To commit murder is to despise the image of God in another human being, something highly offensive to a holy God. **A thief** is also condemned by all. Persons without regard for the property of others are a threat to good order and should be punished. To steal is to reject what Jesus called the second greatest commandment, to love one's neighbor as oneself (Mark 12:31). **An evildoer** is a more general term that includes all kinds of felonies or criminal actions. For a Christian to commit any criminal trespass is to tarnish the name of Christ. **A meddler** is a difficult term to translate because it occurs only here in the New Testament and was rare in secular Greek. "Busybody" and "mischief maker" have also been suggested as translations. Nobody likes a nosy neighbor, and Christians who get in trouble because they haven't minded their own business have only themselves to blame.

In verse 16 Peter returned to the theme of undeserved suffering. He had mentioned verbal abuse in verse 14; the one who **suffers as a Christian** endures physical punishment, such as beating or imprisonment. Peter's use of the term **Christian** is interesting and perhaps surprising, for the term appears in the New Testament only three times (see also Acts 11:26; 26:28). The term means a follower of Christ or someone loyal to Christ. In other words, to be a Christian is not so much to be identified with a *religion* as it is to be identified with the *person of Christ*.

If for bearing **that name** (Christ's) a believer suffers, he **should not be ashamed** (see Acts 5:41; 9:16). Instead a believer should **glorify God,** praising Him for the privilege of suffering for the name of Christ.

What lasting truths are in these verses?

1. God's plan for some believers is that they endure insults and injury for Him.

2. Christians who suffer for doing criminal activities bring shame on Christ's name.

3. When Christians are persecuted, they are being tested and blessed by God.

4. A proper understanding of suffering includes rejoicing and praising God whenever ridicule for Christ's sake occurs.

Trust God and Do Right (1 Pet. 4:19)

*How did Peter summarize his view of Christian suffering? Why did He focus on God as the **Creator** rather than on Christ as the Savior?*

Verse 19: So those who suffer according to God's will should, in doing good, entrust themselves to a faithful Creator.

This single verse summarizes in a nutshell Peter's teaching about persecution and suffering. What he affirmed as true for first-century believers is equally true for 21st-century believers.

1. *Some but not all will suffer.* Peter mentioned **those who suffer,** clearly implying that not all will go through this. Christian history confirms this pattern to be true.

2. *Suffering is never accidental.* It is **according to God's will**—which means that there are divine limits to how severe the suffering will be and how long it will last.

3. *Suffering should be an incentive to do good deeds.* Rather than becoming disheartened and quitting, suffering believers should keep on **doing good.**

4. *Sufferers should trust God more firmly than ever.* Because suffering results in good (as a purifying experience) and makes believers more like Jesus, we should depend on Him rather than panic whenever suffering comes.

5. *Our Creator is faithful in times of suffering.* Because God is the **Creator,** He is powerful enough to direct all the events that happen. Since He made the universe and providentially sustains it, we should never wonder whether He has the ability to deal with the evil forces that come against us as Christians. Because God is **faithful,** He will act in love towards His children. The God in whom Jesus trusted is the same **faithful Creator** we can trust (see Rom. 8:32).

What lasting truths are in these verses?

1. Suffering should be an occasion to keep doing the right thing.
2. Suffering should be an occasion to keep trusting God.

❖ *Spiritual Transformations*

The *Life Question* this lesson seeks to address is, How can I show faithfulness and courage, even when my allegiance to Christ is ridiculed? We have seen Peter's recipe for success even in the face of suffering. Not surprisingly, his insights are profoundly different from the beliefs of secular culture, and those who follow Peter's principles can rest in the assurance of God's approval.

What could you do this week to become more ready to defend your faith? _____
_____

Have you or someone you know suffered persecution as a Christian? How could Peter's teaching have been applied in the situation?
_____
_____

Prayer of Commitment: *Dear God, Thank You for Your wonderful plan that sometimes sends suffering and persecution to Your children. If You have this in store for me, help me to remember that my example is Christ. I want to be able to count it a privilege to suffer for Christ. Amen.*

[1]David Walls and Max Anders, *1 & 2 Peter, 1,2 & 3 John, Jude* in *Holman New Testament Commentary,* vol. 11 (Nashville: Broadman & Holman, 1999), 70.